AF556243

PROMOTION MANAGEMENT

PROMOTION MANAGEMENT

Edited by

J.M. Dewan

&

K.N. Sudarshan

DISCOVERY PUBLISHING HOUSE PVT. LTD.

NEW DELHI-110 002

Published by:
Tilak Wasan
DISCOVERY PUBLISHING HOUSE PVT. LTD.
4831/24, Ansari Road, Prahlad Street
Darya Ganj, New Delhi-110002 (India)
Phone: +91-11-23279245, 43764432
Fax: +91-11-23253475
E-mail: parul.wasan@gmail.com
discoverypublishinghouse@gmail.com
info@discoverypublishinggroup.com
web: www.discoverypublishinggroup.com

***Edition:* 2011**
ISBN: 81-7141-364-1

Promotion Management
Editors

All rights reserved. No part of this publication should be reproduced, stored in a retrieval system, or transmitted in any form or by any means: electronic, mechanical, photocopying, recording or otherwise, without the prior written permission of the author and the publisher.

This book has been published in good faith that the material provided by authors is original. Every effort is made to ensure accuracy of material, but the publisher and printer will not be held responsible for any inadvertent error(s). In case of any dispute, all legal matters are to be settled under Delhi jurisdiction only.

Printed at:
Mehra Offset Press
Delhi

Preface

The management world is in transition. The causes of this transition are many, but the major one is the vast changes in knowledge and in the information that flows in and out of organizations. This changing information disrupts traditions, established processes, well-known procedures, and routine ways of doing things. New principles, concepts, techniques, ideas, expressions, processes, and procedures are emerging, moving us to a new plateau of professional practice. Trying to capture this changing knowledge and information is like trying to capture the atmosphere. How can you do it when the atmosphere is continually shifting and when you need the atmosphere to do the capturing? The best we can do is find a peak from which we can at least get a perspective on management as a whole, decide on the work and responsibilities of management, and gather in whatever practical management information we can. A team of experts in this series represent some of the best contemporary thinking and information available. They represent many major successful corporations, active consulting agencies, and well-known educational institutions, and all are experts on what is happening with the flow of knowledge and information in the management world. This is a lofty pinnacle from which to survey the management world.

Managers and supervisors clamor for current information and guidelines to help solve formidable problems in their work world—problems that range from "how to do it" to "how to resolve conflict when doing it." Many problems are generated from miscommunication and incompetence. As the management practice proceeds from the complex to the supercomplex, problem solving becomes a large-scale challenge requiring new knowledge and skills. Managers and supervisors cannot wait for research breakthroughs with real-world answers to solve these dilemmas. They must tackle them here and now with the useful information and proven practices immediately available. Whether making a decision, solving a problem setting up a procedure, designing a process, or resolving a behaviour conflict, a manager must rely heavily on information. To a great extent, management practitioners are information workers; that is, they generate, distribute, store, retrieve, and consume information. Competence in finding and using the right information at the needed time determines to a considerable extent competence in the management function, activity, or responsibility. The *DPH Management Series* attempts to fill this need for usable information in spite of the changing nature of its subject.

The *DPH Management Series* not a book to be read and later discarded. It is a reference book, a tool to be used by managerial personnel in the day-to-day work of an organization. Like a tool, it should never be more than a reach away when a new situation emerges that demands its use. This series aim to achieve a first-and practical and proven knowledge and information as a self-development opportunity for those who are moving into or upward in management. A complete spectrum of management subjects is immediately available for orientation, study, analysis, assimilation, and problem solving. Within one set of covers is the view of management as a totality. The management field is loaded with ideas that the organization of this handbook series unique logic. It follows both levels and areas of responsibilities of an organization.

The work of this handbook series is the collaborative effort of many outstanding people in the management field. The motivation for this work varied from individual to individual, but the central motivation that united us all was the excitement of capturing the management state-of-the-art and sharing it with colleagues in the dynamic profession of management.

This series should be of great help to managerial practitioners at any organizational level who are responsible for a function, department, or set of responsibilities. The handbook series will also give these practitioners insights into management roles and approaches in other areas as well. The subject matter encompasses top, middle, and lower management. Special emphasis was placed on managing people, time, space, budgets, and resources to give the handbook extra utility for middle and lower management. Students of management in university or educational institutions will find the series an invaluable resource for adding "real world" practices to their academic and theoretical foundations. MBA students will gain an invaluable overview of the total organization to complement their MBA degree. Administrators and public managers can become acquainted with practices employed by managers and supervisors in private organizations. These practices are not always directly applicable in public sector bodies, but with thought and modifications, these private practices can adapt to public organizations. Public and university librarians will find the handbook an indispensable reference for the multitude of questions on many topics from the general public, special groups, associations, and students.

Editors

Contents

1 Promotion–Introduction

Promotion is communicating information between seller an potential buyer-to influence attitudes and behaviour. The marketing manager's promotion job is to tell target customers that the right Product is available at the right place at the right Price.

What the marketing manager communicates is determined when the target customers needs and attitudes are know. How the messages are delivered treated as just another kind of advertising-and often isn't used as effectively as it could be. Publicity deserves much more attention in the future.

Sales promotion refers to promotion activities-other than advertising, publicity and personal selling-that stimulate interest, trial, or purchase by final customers or others in the channel. Sales promotion may be aimed at consumers, at middlemen, or even at a firm's own employees. Examples include coupons, samples of consumer products, special sweepstakes and contests and

Aimed at final Consumers or users	Aimed at middlemen	Aimed at company's on sales force
Banners	Price deals	Contests
Steamers	Promotion allowances	Bonuses
Samples	Sales contests	Meetings
Calendars	Calendars	Promotions
Point-of-purchase materials	Gifts	Displays
Aisle displays	Trade shows	Sales aids
Contests	Meetings	Training materials
Coupons	Catalogs	
Trade shows	Merchandising aids	
Trading camp		

displays at trade shows. Other examples are listed above.

We will talk more about sales promotion later. First however, you need to understand the role of the whole promotion blend-personal selling, mass selling, and sales promotion combined-so you can see how promotion fits into the rest of the marketing mix.

Which methods to use depends on promotion objectives

The different promotion methods can all be viewed as different forms of communication. But good marketers aren't interested in just "communicating". They want to communicate information that will encourage customers to choose their product. They know that if they have better offering, informed customers are more likely to buy. Therefore, they are interested in

(1) reinforcing present attitudes that might lead to favorable behaviour or (2) actually changing the attitudes and behaviour of the firm's target market in terms of demand curves, promotion may help the firm make its present demand curve more inelastic-or shift the demand curve to the right-Informing, persuading, and reminding are basic promotion objectives

Informing, persuading, and reminding are basic promotion objectives

For a firm's promotion to be effective, its promotion objectives must be clearly defined-because the right promotion blend depends on what the firm wants to accomplish. It's helpful to think of three basic promotion objectives: wants to accomplish. It's helpful to think of three basic promotion objectives: informing, persuading, and reminding target customers about the company and its marketing mix. All are concerned with affecting behaviour by providing more information.

Even more useful is a more specific set of promotion objectives that states exactly who you want to inform, persuade, or remind, and why. But this is unique to each company's strategy-and too detailed to discuss here. Instead. We will limit ourselves to the three basic promotion objectives-and how you can reach them.

Informing is educating

Potential customers must know something about a product if they are to buy at all. Therefore, informing may be the most important objective.

For example, a cable TV company found that whenever it offered service to a new neighborhood, most of the families subscribed. The cable company's main job was informing prospects that cable was available.

A firm with a really new product may not have to do anything but inform consumers about it-and show that it works better than other products. When Compaq introduced its "IBM compatible" portable computer, the uniqueness of the product simplified the promotion job. And compaq had the highest ever first year sales for a new company about $11 million. Excitement about the product also generated a lot of free publicity in computer magazines.

Persuading usually becomes necessary

When competitors are offering similar products, however, the firm must not only inform customers that its product is available-but also persuade them to buy it. A persuading objective means the firm will try to develop or reinforce a favourable set of attitudes in the hope of affecting buying behaviour.

Reminding may be enough, sometimes

If target customers already have positive attitudes about the firm's product, then a reminding objective might be suitable. This objective can be extremely important in some cases. Even though customers have been attracted and sold once, they are still targets for competitors appeals. Reminding them of their past satisfaction may keep them from shifting to a competitor. Campbell realizes that the most people know about its soup-so much of its advertising is intended to remind.

Promotion requires effective communication

Promotion must get the attention of the target audience-and communicate effectively-or it's wasted effort. However, this isn't always easy to do. Much promotion doesn't really communicate. You might listen to the radio for hours without really being aware of the ads. Promotional communication can break down in many ways.

The same message may be interpreted differently

Different audiencos may see the same message in different ways-or interpret the same words differently. Such differences are often found in international marketing when translation is a problem. General Motors, for example, had trouble in Puerto Rico with its Nova car. It discovered that, while Nove means "star" in Spanish-when spoken it sounds like "no va", meaning doesn't go". The company changed the car's name to "caribe"-and it sold well.

Semantic problems in the same language may not be so obvious-and yet the negative effects can still be serious. For example, a new children's cough syrup was advertised as "extra strength." The advertising people thought that would assure parents that the product worked well. But cautious mothers avoided the product because they feared that it might be too strong for their children.

Feedback improves communication process

There are many reasons why a message can be misunderstood-or not heard at all. To understand this, it's useful to think about a whole communication process-which means a source trying to reach a receiver with a message. Here we see that a source-the sender of a message-is trying to deliver a message to a receiver-a potential customer. Research shows that customers evaluate not only the message-but also the source of the message-in terms evaluate not only the message-but also the source of the message-in terms of trustworthiness and credibility. For example, information coming from Chrysler Chairman Lee lacocca might be viewed as more impressive than the same message from a junior sales rep.

A source can use many message channels to deliver a message. The personal salesperson does it with voice and action. Advertising must do it with mass media-magazine, newspapers, radio, and TV.

A major advantage of personal selling is that the source-the seller-can get immediate feedback from the receiver. It's easier to judge how the message is being received-and change if it necessary. Mass sellers must depend on marketing research or total sales figures for feedback-and that can take too long.

The noise is any distraction that reduces the effectiveness of the communication process. Conversations during TV and are "noise." Advertisers planning messages must recognize that many possible distractions-noise-can interface with communications.

Encoding and decoding depend on common frame of reference

The basic difficulty in the communication process occurs during encoding and decoding. Encoding is the source deciding what it wants to say and translating it into words or symbols that will have the same meaning to the receiver. Decoding is the receiver translating the message. This process can be very tricky. The meanings of various words and symbols may differ, depending on the attitudes and experiences of the two groups. People need a common frame of references to communicate effectively.

Maidenform encountered this problem with its promotion aimed at working women. The company ran a series of ads depicting women stockbrokers and doctors wearing Maidenform lingerie. The men in the ads were fully dressed Maidenform was trying to show women in positions of authority, but some women felt the ad presented them as sex objects. In this case, the promotion people who encoded the message didn't understand the attitudes of the target market-and how they would decode the message.

Message channel is important, too

The communication process is complicated even more because the receiver is aware that the message is not only coming from a source but also coming through some message channel-the carrier of the message. The receiver may attach more value to a product if the message comes in a well-respected newspaper or magazine, rather than over the radio. Some consumers buy products that are advertised in *Good housekeeping* magazine, for example, because they have faith in its "seal of approval."

Adoption processes can guide promotion planning

The adoption process is related to effective communication and promotion planning. Your learned the six steps in this adoption process: awareness, interest, evaluation, trial, decision, and confirmation. We saw consumer buying as a problem-solving processing which buyers go through these six steps on the way to adopting an idea or product.

Now we see that the three basic promotion objectives are related to these six steps. Informing and persuading may be needed to affect the potential customer's knowledge and attitudes about a product-and then bring about its adoption. Later, promotion can simply remind the customer about that favourable experience-and confirm the adoption decision.

The AIDA model is a practical approach

The basic adoption process fits very neatly with another action-oriented model-called AIDA-which we will use in this and the next two chapters to guide some of our discussion.

The AIDA model consists of four promotion jobs-(1) to get attention (2) to hold interest, (3) to arouse Desire, and (4) to obtain Action.

Getting attention is necessary to make consumers award of the company's offering. Holding interest gives the communication a chance to build the consumer's interest in the product. Arousing desire affects the evaluation process-perhaps building preference. And obtaining action includes gaining trial, which then may lead to a purchase decision. Continuing promotion is needed to confirm the decision-and encourage additional purchases.

Good communication varies promotion blends along adoption curve

The AIDA and adoption processes look at individuals. This emphasis on individuals helps us understand how people behave. But it's also useful to look at markets as a whole. Different customers within a market may behave differently-with some taking the lead in trying new products and, in turn, influencing others.

Adoption curve focuses on market segments, not individuals

Research on how markets accept new ideas has led to the adoption curve model. The adoption curve shows when different groups accept ideas. It shows the need to change the promotion effort as time passes. It also emphasizes the relations among groups-and shows that some groups act as leaders in accepting a new idea.

Innovators don't mind taking some risk

The innovators are the first to adopt. They are eager to try a new idea and willing to take risks. Innovators tend to be young and well educated. They are likely to be mobile-and have many contacts outside their local social group and community. Business firms in the innovator group usually are large and rather specialized. They are seeking new ways to be more effective.

An important characteristic of innovators is that they rely on impersonal and scientific information sources-or other innovators-rather than personal sales people. They often read articles in technical publications or informative ads in special-interest magazines or newspapers.

Early adopters are often opinion leaders

Early adopter are well respected their peers-and often are opinion leaders. They tend to be younger, more mobile, and more creative than later adopters. But unlike innovators, they have fewer contacts outside their own social group or community. Business firms in this category also tend to be specialized.

This group tends to have the greatest contact-of all the groups-with salespeople. Mass media are important information sources, too. Marketers should be very concerned with attracting and selling the early adopter group. Their acceptance is really important in reaching the next group-because the early majority book to the early adopters for guidance. The early adopters can help the promotion effort-by spreading word-of-mouth information and advice among other consumers.

Early majority group is deliberate

The early majority avoid risk and wait to consider a new idea after many early adopters have tried it-and liked it. By the time members of this group start to buy, a product is probably in the market growth stage of the product life cycle and headed for success-if this group buys.

Average-sized business firms that are less specialized often fit in this category. If successful companies in their industry adopt the new idea, they will too.

The early majority have a great deal of contact with mass media, salespeople, and early adopter opinion leaders. Members usually aren't opinion leaders

Late majority is cautious

The late majority are cautious about new ideas. Often they are older than the early majority group-and more set in their ways. So they are less likely to follow opinion leaders and early adopters. In fact, strong social pressure from their own peer group may be needed before they adopt a new product.

Business firms in this group tend to be conservative, similar-sized firms with little specialization.

The late majority make little use of marketing sources of information-mass media and salespeople. They tend to be oriented more to other late adopters rather than to outside sources they don't trust.

Laggards or non-adopters bang on to tradition

Laggards or non-adopters prefer to do things the

way they have been done in the past and are very suspicious of new ideas. They tend to be older and less well educated. They may also be low in social status and income.

The smallest businesses with the least specialization are often in this category. They cling to the status quo and think it's the safe way. They don't realize that other companies are searching for better ways of doing things. The laggards stay the same-while competitors are adopting new ideas.

The main source of information for laggards is other laggards. This certainly is bad news for marketers who are trying to reach a whole market quickly- who want to use only one promotion method. In fact, it may not pay to bother with this group.

Opinion leaders help spread the word

Adoption curve research supports our earlier discussion the importance of opinion leaders-people who influence other people's attitudes and behaviour. It shows the importance of early adopters. They influence the early majority-and help spread the word to many others.

Marketers know the importance of these personal conversations and recommendations by opinion leaders. If early groups reject the product, it may never get off the ground. For example, some movie goers are usually among the first to see new movies. If they think a movie is dull, they are quick to tell their friends not to waste their time and money.

But if they accept a product, then what the opinion leaders in each social group say about it can be very important. This "word-of mouth" publicity may do the real selling job-long before the customer ever walks into the retail store. Some companies try to target promotion to encourage opinion leadership. When Canon introduced a high-quality new "automatic" 35 mm camera, it prepared special ads designed to help opinion leaders explain to others how the camera worked. Other advertisers take a simpler approach. They just say "tell your friends."

We know less about the adoption process in industrial markets. It seems likely that the same general process is work-but there is less word-of-mouth communication in these markets. This makes both personal selling and mass selling more important in communicating with industrial buyers and all the multiple buying influences.

May need a different blend for beach product market segment

Each unique market segment may need a separate marketing mix-and a different promotion blend. Some mass selling specialists have missed this point. They think mainly in mass marketing"-rather than "target marketing terms. Aiming at large markets may be desirable in some situations, but promotion aimed at everyone can end up hitting no one. In developing the promotion blend. You should be especially careful not to slip into a "shotgun approach when what you really need is a "rifle" approach-with a more careful aim.

Successful promotion may be an economical blend

Once promotion objectives for a strategy are set, a marketing manager will probably use a blend of promotion methods-since some jobs can be done more economically one way than another. You can see this most clearly in industrial markets. While personal selling dominates most industrial promotion budgets, mass selling is necessary,, too. Personal sales representatives nearly always have to complete the sale, but it is seldom practical for them to carry the whole promotion load. The cost of an industrial sales call is about $240. This relatively high cost is because salespeople have only limited time and they spend much of it on non-selling activities-traveling, paper work, sales meetings, and strictly service calls. Less than half of their time is available for actual selling.

The job of reaching all the buying influences is made more costly and difficult by the constant turnover of buyers and influences. An industrial salesperson may be responsible for several hundred customers and prospects-with many buying influences per company. He doesn't have enough time to get the company's whole message across to every potential customer. A firm invests too much in a salesperson to use his time and skill answering questions that could be better handled through mass selling. It may cost an industrial advertiser much less than a dollar per reader to advertise in a trade magazine to a targeted group of possible buyers or influencers. After the mass selling does the ground work, the salesperson can concentrate on answering specific questions-and closing the sale.

Factors affecting the selection of a promotion blend

Most business firms develop a promotion blend of some kind-because the three promotion methods complement each other. But what blend is right in a particular situation?

Each promotion blend should be designed to achieve the firm's promotion objectives in each marketing strategy. The particular blend a firm selects also depends on other factors-including (1) the promotion budget available. (2) stage of product in its life cycle, (3) nature of competition, (4) target of the promotion, and (5) the nature of the product.

Size of promotion budget affects promotion efficiency

There are some economies of scale in promotion, And ad on network TV might cost less per person reached than an ad on local TV. Similarly, city-wide radio. TV, and newspapers may be cheaper than nighbourhood newspaper or direct personal contact. But the total cost for some "mass media" may force small firms-or those with small promotion budgets-to use promotion alternatives that are more expensive per contact. For example, a small retailer might want to use local television but find that he has only enough money for an ad in the Yellow Pages-and an occasional newspaper ad.

When the promotion budget is limited, sales promotion and direct mail may be attractive possibilities. Direct mail selling can be carefully targeted to the desired target market-so there is little wasted expense. Some companies, like Radio

Shack, try to get the name and address of every customer to build their own mailing lists. This is easy to do when most customers pay by check or credit card. Computerized mailing lists can also be purchased very inexpensively. For less than 5 cents a name, a company selling medical supplies can buy a list of all the doctors in certain ZIP Code areas-with the names printed on mailing labels. Thousands of such specific lists are available. Most special interest magazines sell their subscription lists.

Stage of product in various life cycle

A new product seldom becomes a spectacular success overnight. The adoption curve helps explain why. Further, the product must go through the product life cycle stages, that described market introduction, market growth, market maturity, and sales decline. During these stages, promotion blends may have to change to achieve different promotion objectives.

Market introduction state-"this new idea is good"

During market introduction, the basic promotion objective is informing. If the product is a really new idea, the promotion must build primary demand-demand for the general product idea-for example, portable telephones or laser printers for computers-not just the company's own brand. There may be few potential innovators during the introduction stage, and personal selling can help find them Salespeople also are needed to find good channel members-and persuade them to carry the new product. Sales promotion may be targeted at salespeople or channel members to get them interested in selling the new product. And sales promotion may also encourage customers to try it.

Market growth stage-"our brand is best"

In the market growth stage, more competitors enter the market and promotion emphasis shifts from building primary demand to stimulating selective demand-demand for a company's own brand. The main job is to persuade customers to buy-and keep buying-the company's product.

Now that more potential customers are trying and adopting the product, mass selling may become more economical. But personal salespeople must still work in the channels-expanding the number of outlets.

Market maturity stage-"our brand is better, really"

In the market maturity stage, more competitors have entered the market. Promotion becomes more persuasive. At this stage, mass selling and sales promotion may dominate the promotion blends of consumer products firms. Industrial products may require more aggressive personal selling-perhaps supplemented by more advertising. The total dollars allocated to promotion may rise as competition increases.

If a firm already has high sales-relative to competitors-it may have a real advantage in promotion at this stage. If, for example, Nabisco has twice the sales for a certain type of cookie as Keebler, its smaller competitor, and they both spend the same percentage of total sales on promotion-Nabisco will be spending twice as much and will probably communicate to more people.

Nabisco may get even more than twice as much promotion because of economies of scale.

Firms that have strong brands are bale to use reminder-type advertising at this stage-to be sure customer remember the product name. This may be much less expensive than persuasive efforts.

Sales decline stage-let's tell those who still want our product

During the sales decline stage, the total amount spent on promotion usually decreases-as firms try to cut costs to remain profitable. Since some people may still want the product, firms need more targeted promotion to reach these customers.

On the other hand, some firms may increase promotion to try to slow the cycle-at least temporarily. Crayola had almost all of the market for children's crayons, but sales had been slowly declining as new kinds of markers came along. Crayola slowed the cycle with more promotion spending and a message to parents to buy their kids a fresh box.

Nature of competition requires different promotion

Firms in monopolistic competition may favour mass selling-because they have differentiated their marketing mixes have something to talk about. As a market tends toward pure competition-or oligopoly-it is difficult to predict what will happen. Competitors in some markets try to out-promote each other. The only way for a competitor to stay in this kind of market is to match rivals' promotion efforts-unless the whole marketing mix can be improved in some other way. We see a lot of such competitive advertising in our daily newspapers-and in "cents-off" coupons at grocery store check-out counters.

In markets that are drifting toward pure competition, some check-out counters, to price cutting. Lower prices may be offered to middlemen, customers or both. This may increase the number of units sold-temporarily-but it may also repetitive relation may reduce and the amount available for promotion per unit. And competitive retaliation may reduce the temporary sales gains-and drag price levels down faster. The cash flowing into the business may decline-and promotion may have to be cut back.

Target of promotion helps set the blend

Promotion can be directed to five different groups: final consumers, industrial customers, retailers, wholesalers, and even a company's own employees. The right promotion blend for each group can be different.

Promotion to final consumers

The large number of potential customers almost forces producers of consumer products and retailers to emphasize mass selling and sales promotion. Sales promotion-such as contests or free contests or free samples-may build consumer interest and short-term sales of a product. Effective mass selling may build enough brand familiarity so that little personal selling is needed-as in self-service and discount operations.

Personal selling can be effective, too. Some retailers-specially shops in particular-rely heavily on well-informed salespeople. But aggressive personal selling to final consumers usually is found only in relatively expensive channel systems, such as those for fashionable clothing and furniture.

Promotion to industrial customers

Industrial customers are much less numerous than final consumers-and there is more reason to emphasize personal selling. Industrial customers may have technical questions-or need adjustments in the marketing mix. Producers' or wholesaler sales reps can be more flexible in adjusting their companies appeals to suit each customer. They also are able to call back later-and provide confirmation and additional information. Personal selling becomes more practical as the size of each purchase increases. And larger unit purchases are more typical in industrial markets.

When it is hard to identify all of the companies-or even industries-that might use a product, ads in trade publications can inform potential customers that the product is available and stimulate inquiries. Then a salesperson can follow up.

Promotion to retailers

As with industrial buyers, the relatively small number of retailers makes it practical for producers and wholesalers to emphasize personal selling. Sales promotion-such as contests that offer vacation trips for high-volume retailers and some mass selling in trade magazines can be valuable. But most of the promotion is done by salespeople. They can answer retailers' questions about what promotion will be directed toward the final consumer, the retailers' own part in selling the product, and important details on prices, markups, and promotion assistance and allowances.

Much promotion to retailers is concerned with informing. But since the producer's or wholesaler's sales reps cannot guarantee the retailer a profit, the promotion must also be persuasive. The sales rep must convince the retailer that demand for the product exists-and that making a profit will be easy. Further, the rep must establish and maintain good channel relationships. Retailers must be convinced that the producer or wholesaler has their interests at hear.

Another reason personal selling is so important in dealing with retailers is that marketing mixes may have to be adjusted from one geographic territory in another-to meet competitive situations. The mixes in highly competitive urban areas, for example, may emphasize price more than those in outlying areas.

Promotion to wholesalers

Promotion to wholesalers is very similar to promotion to retailers-except that wholesalers are less numerous and perhaps even more aware of demand and cost. They respond the economic arguments. They want to know about the promotion the producer intends to direct at final customers and retailers. They also want personal attention from producers sales reps-to be certain that any producers sales reps-to be certain that any problems will be handled promptly. A good sales rep helps to cement the relationship between producer and wholesaler.

Promotion to employees

Some companies put a lot of emphasis on promotion to employees especially salespeople. Sales promotions-like contests that give free trips to big sellers-are common in many businesses. And some large companies are trying to design ads targeted at customers that also communicate to employees-and boost the employees' image. This is especially important in service-oriented industries where the quality of the employees' efforts is a big part of the product. General Motors, for example, promotes "Mr. Good wrench"-the well-qualified mechanic who provides friendly, expert service. The ad communicates primarily to customers-bit it also reminds service people that what they do is important and appreciated.

Nature of the produce makes a big difference

The target customers; view of the product is the common thread that ties together all the variables in a marketing mix. The customers' view of the product affects the promotion blend, too. The product classes have a direct bearing on the place objectives. These product classes influence the development of promotion blends, too. The way will consider the impact of some general product characteristics on promotion blends.

Technical nature of product

An extremely technical industrial product may require a heavy emphasis on personal selling-using technically trained salespeople. This is the only sure way to make the product understood-and get feedback on how customers use it. The technical sales rep meets with engineers, plant people, purchasing agents, and top managers-and can adjust the sales message to the needs of these various influences.

Mass selling, on the other hand, is practical for many consumer products because there is no technical story to be told. If there are some technical details-for example, with cars or appliances-they can be offered to interested customers-perhaps in sales promotion materials at the retailer's showroom.

Degree on brand familiarity

If a product has already won brand preference or insistence-perhaps after years of satisfactory service-aggressive personal selling may not be needed. Reminder-type advertising may be all that's necessary. Hershey Chocolae long prided itself on not having to do any advertising! In the last 10 years, however, increased competition in the United States has forced Hershey to begin using advertising and sales promotion. In Canada-where it is not well established-Hershey always has advertised aggressively.

If a producer has not differentiated its product and brand, and does not intend to build brand familiarity-perhaps because of a small budget-then much heavier emphasis on personal makes sense. The objective is to build good channel relations- and encourage channel members to recommend the product.

How typical promotion budgets are blended

There is no one right blend

There is no one right promotion blend for all situation. Each one must be developed as pert of a marketing mix. But to round out our discussion of promotion blends, let's look at some typical ways promotion budgets are spread across the three promotion methods.

The percentage of total promotion budgets spent on personal selling, advertising, and sales promotion in various situations. The wholesalers rely on personal selling almost exclusively, while a producer of branded consumer products spends about equally on mass selling to consumers, personal selling and sales promotion to middlemen and consumers. On the other hand, smaller producers and firms that offer relatively undifferentiated consumer products or industrial products put more emphasis on personal selling, with the rest of the budget going mainly to sales promotion. Note that here we are referring to percentages not the level of expenditures.

Less is spent on advertising or sales promotion than on personal selling

Many people think that most promotion money is spent on advertising because advertising is all around them. But, it guessed-correctly-that personal selling gets heavier emphasis. And sales promotion is important; too. The many ads you see in magazines and newspapers and on TV are impressive-and costly. But all the special sales promotions-coupons, sweepstakes, trade shows, sporting events sponsored by firms, and the like-add up to almost the same amount of money. Similarly, most retail sales are completed by salesclerks. And behind the scenes, much personal selling goes on the channels. In total, personal selling is several times more expensive than mass selling or sales promotion.

Someone must plan and manage the promotion blend

Selecting a promotion blend is a strategic decision that should fit with the rest of a marketing strategy. Once a firm sets the outlines of its promotion blend, it must develop and implement more detailed plans for the parts of the blend. This is the job of specialists-such as sales managers and advertising managers.

Sales managers manage salespeople

Sales managers are concerned with managing personal selling. Often the sales manager is responsible for building good distribution channels and implementing Place policies. In smaller companies, the sales manager may also as the marketing manager-and the responsible for advertising and sales promotion too. Since most sales managers have come up through sales, they usually know more about he power of personal contact. This can be both a strength and a weakness. They may believe in-and be able to develop and motivate-an effective sales force. But they may have less interest in-and respect for-developing a whole promotion blend.

Advertising managers work with ads and agencies

Advertising managers manager their company's mass selling effort in television, newspapers, magazines, and other media. Their job is choosing the right media-and developing the ads. Advertising departments within their own firms may help in these efforts-or they may use outside advertising agencies. They-or their agencies-may handle publicity, too. Or it may be handled by whoever handles public relations-communication with non-customers-including labour, public interest groups, stockholders, and the government.

Advertising managers usually come up through advertising-and many have an exaggerated view of its potential power. They may think that advertising can do one whole promotion job-or that advertising is promotion.

Sales promotion managers need many talents

Sales promotion managers manage their company's sales promotion effort. They fill the gaps between the sales and advertising managers-increasing their effectiveness. In some companies sales promotion managers have independent status, reporting to the marketing manager. Sometimes the sales promotion effort is handled by the sales or advertising departments. But sales promotion activities are so varied that firms use both inside and outside specialists. If a firm's sales promotion expenses exceed those for advertising, it probably should have a separate sales promotion manager.

Marketing manager talks to all, blends all

Because of differences in outlook and experience, the advertising, sales, and sales promotion managers may have trouble working with each other as partners or equals. This is especially true when each feels that his own approach is the most important. The marketing manager must weigh the pros and cons of the various methods. Then the must come up with an effective promotion blend-fitting in the various departments and personalities and coordinating their efforts.

To be able to evaluate a company's promotion blend, you must first know more about the individual areas of promotion decisions. We start in the direction in the next section-with more discussion of sales promotion.

Sale promotion: Do something different to stimulate change

Sales promotion refers to those promotion activities-other than advertising, publicity, and personal selling-that stimulate interest, trial, or purchase by final customers or others in the channel. Sales promotion generally tries to complement to other promotion methods. And, if properly done, it can be very effective. But there are problems in the sales promotion area.

Sales promotion is a weak spot in marketing

Sales promotion is often a weak spot in marketing. The sales promotion includes a wide variety of activities-each of which may be custom-designed and used only once. Thus the typical company develops little skill in sales promotion.

Mistakes caused by lack of experience can be very costly, too. One promotion sponsored jointly by Polaroid and Trans World Airlines proved to be a disaster. The promotion offered a coupon worth 25 percent off the price of any TWA ticket with the purchase of a $20 Polaroid camera. The companies intended to appeal to vacationers who take pictures when they travel. Instead, travel agents bought up many of the cameras. For the price of the $20 camera, they made an extra 25 percent on every TWA ticket they sold. And big companies bought thousands of the cameras-to save on overseas travel expenses.

Sales promotion problems are likely to be worse when a company has no sales promotion managers. If the personal selling or advertising managers are responsible for sales promotion, they often treat it as a stepchild." They allocate money to sales promotion if there is any "left over"-or a crisis develops. Many companies-even some large ones-don't have a separate budget for sales promotion-or even know what it costs in total.

Making sales promotion work is a learned skill-not a sideline for amateurs. In fact, specialists in sales promotion have developed-both inside larger and as outside consultants. Some are extremely creative and might be willing to take over the whole promotion job. But it is the marketing manager's responsibility set promotion objectives and policies that will fit in with the rest of each marketing strategy.

Sales promotion spending is big-and getting bigger

This need for sales promotion experts-and perhaps separate status for sales promotion within the marketing organization-is apparent when we consider how much money is involved. Sales promotion expenditures were estimated to be $75 billion in 1986. That's almost as much as the total amount spent on advertising.

Spending on sales promotion is growing-sometimes at the expense of other promotion methods-for several reasons. Sales promotion has proved successful in increasingly competitive markets. Sales promotion can usually be implemented quickly-and gets results sooner than advertising. It is often designed to get action. Act media-a New York firm specializing in sales promotion-sent representatives to 4, 800 stores around the country, where thy gave away booklets of coupons for a variety of products. About 12 percent of the coupons were quickly redeemed-nearly half for products the shopper didn't ordinarily buy.

Sales promotion activities also help a product manager win support from an already overworked sales force. The sales force may be especially receptive to sales promotion-including promotion in the channels because competition is growing and middlemen respond to sales promotion. The sales reps can see that their company is willing to help them win more business.

Earlier, we noted that sales promotion can be aimed at final consumers or users, channel members, and company employees. Let's look at some of the sales promotion tools used for these different target receivers-and what they are expected to accomplish.

Sales promotion for final consumers or users

Sales promotion aimed at final consumers or users usually is trying to increase demand or speed up the time of purchase. Such promotion might involve developing materials to be displayed in retailers' stores-including banners and streamers, sample packages, calendars, and various point-of-purchase materials. The sales promotion people also might develop the aisle displays for supermarkets. They might be responsible for "sweepstakes" displays for supermarkets. They might be responsible for "sweepstakes" contests-as well as coupons designed to get customers to buy a product by a certain date.

All of these efforts are aimed at specific promotion objectives. For example, the customers already have a favorite brand, it may be hard to get them to try anything new. Or it may take a while for them to become accustomed to a different product. A free sample tube of toothpaste might be just what it takes to get cautious consumers to try-and like-a new product. Such samples might be distributed house to house, by mail, at stores, or attached to other products sold by the firm.

Sales promotion directed at industrial customers might use the same kinds of ideas. In addition, the sales promotion people might set up and staff trade show exhibits. Here, attractive models are often used to encourage buyers to look at a firm's product-especially when it is displayed near other similar products in a circus-like atmosphere.

Some industrial sellers give promotion items-pen sets, cigarette lighters, watches, or more expensive items-to "remind industrial customers of their products. This is common practice in many industries. But it can be a sensitive area, too. Some companies do not allow buyers to take any gift-of any kind-from a supplier. They fear the buyer's judgement may be influenced by the supplier who gives the best promotion items!

Sales promotion for middlemen

Sales promotion aimed at middlemen-sometimes called trade promotion-stresses price-related matters. The objective may be to encourage middlemen to stock new items, buy in larger quantity, or buy early. The tools used here are price and/or merchandise allowances, promotion allowances, and perhaps sales contests to encourage retailers or wholesalers to sell specific items-or the company's whole line. Offering to send contest winners to Hawali, for example, may increase sales greatly.

Sales promotion for own employees

Sales promotion aimed at the company's own sales force might try to encourage getting new customers, selling a new product, or selling the company's whole line. Depending on the objectives, the tools might be contests, bonuses on sales or number of new accounts, and holding sales meetings at fancy resorts to raise everyone's spirits.

Ongoing sales promotion work might also be aimed at the sales force-to help sales management. Sales promotion might be responsible for preparing sales portfolios, videotapes on new products, displays, and other sales aids. Sales promotion people might develop the sales training material that the sales force uses in working with customers-and other channel members. They might develop special racks-for product displays-that the sales rep sells or gives to retailers. In other words, rather than expecting each individual sales-person-or the sales manager-to develop these sales aids, sales promotion might be given this responsibility.

Service-oriented firms, such as hotels or restaurants, now use sales promotions targeted at their employees. Some, for example, give a monthly cash prize for the employee who provides the "best service". And the employee's picture is displayed to give recognition.

Promotion is an important part of any marketing mix. Most consumers and intermediate customers can choose from among many products. To be successful, a producer must not only offer a good product at a reasonable price, but also inform potential customers about the product and where they can buy it. Further producers must tell wholesales and retailers in the channel about their product-and their marketing mix. These middlemen, in turn, must use promotion to reach their customers.

The promotion blend should fit logically into the strategy that is being developed to satisfy a particular target market. What should be communicated to them-and how-should be stated as part of the strategy planning.

The overall promotion objective is affecting buying behaviour-but the basic promotion objectives are informing, persuading, and reminding.

Three basic promotion methods can be used to reach these objectives. How the promotion methods are combined to achieve affective communication can be guided by behavioural science findings. In particular, we know something about the communications process and how individuals and groups adopt new products.

An action-oriented framework called AIDA can help guide planning of promotion blends. But the marketing manager has the final responsibility to combining the promotion methods into one promotion blend for each marketing mix. Special factors that may affect the promotion blend are the size of the promotion budget, stage of product in its life cycle, the nature of competition and the nature of the product.

In this chapter, we considered some promotion basics and went into some detail on sales promotion. We will not treat sales promotion further because it is difficult to generalize about all of the possibilities.

2 Sales Promotion

Sales Promotion is the newest element of promotion. As such, its total meaning is still undertermined. Traditionally, it has been viewed as everything that is left over after one accounts for advertising, personal selling, and publicity. Clearly this the hall approach is insufficient if we are to understand this arm of promotion. Even the definition of the American Marketing Associations (AMA) offers little clarity: "Marketing activities, other than personal selling, advertising, and publicity, that stimulate consumer purchasing and dealer effectiveness, such as display, shows and exhibitions, demonstrations, and various non-recurrent selling efforts not in the ordinary routine." In the AMA view, sales promotion supplements both personal selling and advertising, coordinates them, and helps make them more effective. A simpler way of viewing sales promotion is to say that it means special offers. Special in the sense that they are extra as well as because they are specific in time or place:

offers in the sense that they are direct propositions, the acceptance of which forms a deal.

As in most aspects of marketing, the rationale of sales promotion is to provide a direct stimulus to produce a desired response by customers. It is not clear, however, what the distinctions are between sales promotion and advertising, personal selling, and publicity.

Personal salesmanship is the skill, and sales management is the organization of that skill, by which potential buyers are so convinced by another person's argument and methods of persuasion that they decide to buy. The essence of good salesmanship is person-to-person contact,. The weapons the salesperson fights with include sales promotional weapons, and it is often these weapons that finally clinch a deal.

Promotional advertising is the communication of ideas about a firm and its products through the standard commercial media. Some of the content of advertising messages may well be sales promotional in character. Public relations involves the instillation and maintenance of mutual understanding between a firm and all who are likely to come into contact with it. Very little of the make-up of public relations concerns sales promotions, although it can spread the news of a successful scheme by insuring that it gets editorial mention, for instance, Quite often, however, as in the case of fairs and house journals, the borderline between sales promotion and public relations becomes obscure.

Another area where the boundary is not so clear is that of involving product and pricing tactics. Suppose that pillsbury decides to tape three cans of their buttermilk canned biscuits together and is this a banded multipack special offer and therefore promotional? Or is it just an example of a giant-sized economy pack and therefore question has to be asked "Is it intended to be a permanent feature of the manufacturer's product policy to have the family pack as a component of the product?" If it is not it is a sales promotion scheme. The same sort of problem comes up when studying strategies run by firms in service industries. If it is not it is a sales promotion scheme. The same sort of problem comes up when studying strategies run by firms in service industries. If a hotel offers cut-price accommodations at off peak-times of the year. Is it a feature of the hotel management's provides price reductions on tickets to local theaters for their guests, is it part of the product or is it a device to attract customers for a limited period only? Again, the answer can only be given once the question about permanence is asked.

Although industries such as food, drink, tobacco, car, soap and detergent, pharmaceutical, domestic appliance and oil are the best-known users of sales promotion, they are by no means the only ones. The aircraft manufacturing, ship building, engineering, chemical, and retailing industries are also great sales promoters, even though they may not all be also great sales a promoters, is not just confined to consumer goods, although it appears to be more widely used with consumer goods as the casual observer seldom comes into contact with capital goods firms and so tends to think that these techniques are confined to firms making goods sold to the ultimate consumer.

There is little doubt that the growth of sales promotion has been quite substantial during recent years. It is estimated that between 1969 and 1976, sales promotion expenditures grew at a rate of 9.4 percent for advertising. In 1976, the total expenditures on sales promotion exceeded $30 billion, and this trend is expected to continue. On the average, 20-35 percent of a typical company's promotional budget goes towards sales promotion.

There are several possible factors that may have contributed to this dramatic growth.

1. There is a greater acceptance by top management of sales promotion as a sales-generating device.
2. Product managers have learned to implement sales promotion as part of their overall product strategy.
3. There is increased pressure on management to show a faster return on the promotional investment, which sales promotion can do.
4. Inflation and other economic factors have made the appeals of sales promotion more attractive to the average consumer.

5. These same factors have brought greater pressure from middle agents for sales promotion deals.
6. The increased competitive situation has forced companies to look for new advantages in the form of sales promotion.

Reasons for the existence of sales promotion

As will become apparent later, many forms of sales promotion exist. Consequently, it is virtually impossible to establish a standardized set of reasons or objectives that apply to all sales promotion. While the intent of running a cents-off coupon in a local newspaper is intended to stimulate product purchase, free marketing research provided to a wholesaler may have an entirely different purpose. Suffice it to say that the ultimate objective of all sales promotion is to positively influence sales either directly or indirectly. The means for doing this will be discussed later.

Yet, there is a benefit in delineating the advantages sales promotion can offer the marketing manager. Perhaps the greatest strength of sales promotion is that it can be effectively employed by businesses of all sizes. Because sales promotion devices can be relatively inexpensive and easily customized, sales promotion can be used by the smallest of marketers. For example, a small gift shop can easily employ gift vouchers, free samples, special offers, or double-stamp days if they see fit. Conversely, General Motors also uses sales promotion by offering a free audit system to all its dealers. The only limitation on both businesses is their creative skills in designing an appropriate sales promotion vehicle.

A second advantage using sales promotion is its effectiveness in highly competitive market situations. Today, there are extensive choices available to each buyer, not only between brands of the same type of product, but between different types of products providing the same sort of satisfaction. Competition works itself out in the marketplace and particularly at the point of sale where the final deals are made and the act of exchange takes place. It is at the point of sale that a homemaker may actually make her decision on which toilet paper to buy, or a managing director decides whether to accept the terms and conditions of sale of a morality-thousand-pound deal involving capital equipment that will be consumed over many years. Given that in highly competitive markets it is extremely difficult to differentiate one's product in a real way from that of competitors, sales promotion may be the only way a company can be successful. For the furniture store owner, this may mean giving away a ceiling fan with any furniture purchase over $1000. For Colgate-Palmolive it may mean enclosing a free dental hygiene booklet with each tube of Colgate.

The third advantage for sales promotion is closely aligned with the tremendous increase in capital investment found in most industries. Because so many companies are capital intensive today, it is critical that economies of scale be reached in production as soon as possible. As a result, very high levels of production have to be maintained throughout the life of the product. Unfortunately, with increased competition and saturated markets, it is much more difficult to find outlets for these products. Sales promotion has provided a partial solution to this dilemma in two ways. First, it has increased product turnover rates, thus improving the cash flow problem. Second, it has opened new outlet for these surplus products. For example, companies such as Taxes Instruments and Sony have found brand new markets for their products by offering them to companies as part of their employee incentive programs. As a result, thousands of calculators and television sets have been offered as rewards for exceptional service or as prizes for sales contests.

A fourth justification for sales promotion is when an oligopolistic market situation exists. In this situation, just a few companies exist in the market, but competition is very intense between them. In the developed countries, conditions of oligopoly apply in industries such as oil, motor vehicles, aerospace, electrical and chemical products, processed foods, and toiletries, and also in the brewing entries, there is widespread use of sales promotion techniques. In the oil industry, there are the multitude of schemes offered through service stations, special contract terms negotiated with large users of fuel oil, free map and guide services, and so on. In the car industry, trade-in allowances on secondhand cars are customary as is plenty of discounting activity just before the introduction of new models. On the computer side, promotion takes the form of special rental arrangements and the provision of tailor-made software. Banking has become active in sales promotion through techniques such as free advice to customers, competition in deposit rates, money market rates, NOW account rates, bank charges, and the provision of special offers to students, working women, and the elderly.

Why is sales promotion so prevalent in industries that re oligopolistic? The reason is not merely because of the size of each firm, but for this other good reason as well: no firm operating under these conditions likes to compete on price. If price competition arises, every firm is adversely affected because all other firms in the industry have roughly the same costs and are forced to match the price reduction to maintain their market share. One major competitor determining when price changes are to occur-price leadership-is normal practice, even if there is no formal price conspiracy in operation. The only time producers are likely to drop prices is if they believe they have some fairly permanent advantage over their rivals that would make it difficult for them to follow.

Instead of price competition, rivalry takes the form of trying to increase business by expanding the share of market by better distribution, service, salesmanship and promotion. This is particularly true of industries where the total market is more or less static and saturated. It is when the battle is joined for replacement or repeat sales, as well as for competitors' customers, that the sales promotion war really heats up. This also effectively prevents newcomers from breaking into the market easily on a large scale because they cannot afford the selling costs.

As there are only a few firms in an oligopolistic industry for each participant to study, once a competitor's weaknesses become known its rivals are able to exploit them by skillful promotional methods. Then, the promotional battle tends to escalate automatically, especially when budgets are set using competitor's expenditures as a base which must be exceeded. If there were many firms, this situation would not develop so readily. Promotional campaigns can be specifically aimed at competitors' weaknesses, and with much greater effectiveness if an industry consists of only a few firms.

A fifth justification for sales promotion revolves around the perceived high risk the customer associates with committing resources in the purchase of a product. Although there is little evidence that most consumers see individual sales promotional schemes as quite distinct phenomena from the products with which such schemes are associated. That is to say, brand image is affected neither positively nor negatively by the value of a scheme to the buyer. It is simply an extra inducement to buy-its function is to change behavior by providing a stimulus to buy.

Risk felt by potential customers is most likely to be present in the buying situation when:

1. The product is new and untried.

Sales promotional remedy-sampling, demon-stration, trial run, guarantee of benefit. Free trips for customer to visit the factory or other users.

2. Benefits will not be felt or completed for some time.

Sales promotional remedy—delayed invoicing, premium offers, linked services.

3. The buyer is afraid that new products will be launched thus rendering the one bought obsolete before it is fully depreciated.

Sales promotional remedy—leasing agreement with discounts for trading-up, guaranteed buy-back arrangements.

4. The product on its own is not quite perceived to be adequate value-for-money.

Sales promotional remedy—premium offers couponing, collection schemes, and contests.

5. The product will not be compatible with the buyers' consumption system.

Sales promotional remedy—tailor-made package deal, training facilities, container premiums.

The final advantage in sales promotion is the existence of a large number of marginal customers. Marginal customers are those buyers who are almost at the point of purchase but not quite. Every other element of the proposition put to them has been assembled and still the deal has not quite been completed, just an extra push will do it. Sales promotion schemes provide a last-minute and specific inducement that is possible to introduce without disturbing any other element of the deal.

To summarize, sales promotion is no longer viewed as just a supplement to advertising and personal selling. In many instances, sales promotion is the major thrust of the promotional effort. Thus, much of sales promotion is aimed directly at influencing behaviour. It does so by providing a last-minute stimulus to act in one way rather than another. It does not work upon a customer's felt need for a product in itself, neither does it attempt to argue a case: instead, it offers a direct inducement to act by providing extra worth over and above that represented by the permanent bundle of values built into the product at its normal price. It is essentially part of the deal because, by definition, these temporary inducements are offered at the time and place the buying decision is made. They are therefore the last set of influences brought to bear upon sonal sales techniques and packaging as major factors in the decision. This means that promotional inducements are powerful simply because they are the most recent of all influences; they do not need to be remembered; they are direct in their appeal and in the proposition that they make; and above all they seek a favorable response by demanding it.

Sales promotion target markets

The most meaningful way in which to classify

sales promotion techniques is based on target markets. Essentially, three such target markets exist: Consumers, employees and distributors and dealers.

Consumer promotions

The average consumer is always looking for a deal. This is true in respect to all phases of our lives, including jobs, products, and relationships. Sales promotion is effective in attaining that something-for-nothing benefit we are constantly seeking.

It appears that sales promotions tend to be most effective when they are offered as a temporary inducement. Even the most naive consumer becomes skeptical when a retail outer runs a year-long sale. Thus, sales promotions should be offered sparingly and for short durations of time. The following discussion deals with the various types of consumer sales promotion devices.

Price deals price deals are simply a short-term reduction in the price of a product, either nationally or, more usually, locally, in order to stimulate demand that for some reason has fallen off. A scheme like this might include refunds on new products, cents-off coupons, or some type of combination.

If a price offer is going to succeed, the first and most obvious factor to be looked at is the normal brand buying motives of the consumer. The consumer must buy based primarily on price alone for a price offer to be effective in inducing a brand switch. Research indicates that if the consumer buys for any other major reason, dropping the price temporarily will make little difference to sales. The exception would occur in those situations and with those products where brand loyalty is particularly weak and where there are thus a great many marginal buyers always searching across the range of brands. In such a case, a small monetary offer is often enough to persuade people to switch or to remain loyal despite competitive inducements. Let's look at the primary price deals.

Price discount or cents-off deals are probably the oldest type of sales promotion within this category. A price discount is usually apparent only at the point of sale. It is marked on the package and is not usually advertised. Although with evidence in inducing buyers to switch brands, one does find more and more promotions being advertised, particularly in the grocery business. A price offer alone is of little practical use in attracting customers who have never used the product before. They will want to know far more about it than the mere fact that there is three cents off, as the original price and value to them were unknown anyway. Moreover, a price offer does not make existing customers buy more often, but they may buy in larger quantities.

This brings us to another main conclusion about the type of product that a price offer is used to sell. It is not just a product bought often by the same customer and with an elastic demand curve. It is also a product that most people use anyway, and at a offer is usually marked on the package, this type of promotion relies on adequate display for its effectiveness, this accounts for the importance attached to it in self-service stores of all kinds, which rely on massed display.

One particular advantage of a price offer is that it is simple and quick to administer and therefore makes an excellent tactical weapon for quickly countering a competitor's marketing move- whether an advertising campaign, a test market operation. Or a sales promotional scheme of their own. Unfortunately, price offers are also easily countered for the same reason and because of their short-term effectiveness in getting consumers to switch brands impulsively.

Here in one final, but important point before leaving the subject of price offers. Market researchers and others have frequently found that consumers, when other guides are lacking, take price as an indicator of quality. If one is unable to test a new unfamiliar complex, seldom-bought brand of product, it is impossible to learn whether it is worth the money. All one has to fall back on is a rather vague conception of what the price should be, the salesperson's argument, and the price being asked. "The higher the price, the better the quality must be", the potential buyer thinks. " I mean, after all, a high price must reflect high costs; and high costs mean that the quality of the materials and workmanship must be good don't they?" In a situation like this, to offer a promotional price reduction is to inject an element of disturbance into the buyer's set of information. It looks incongruous; almost as if a lowered price says something different from all the other consistent elements of the marketing mix. The buyer may, therefore, reject the proposition, thinking that the offer is inappropriate and possibly that a corner has been cur somewhere or the pack is a specially small one."

Coupon offers may be the tastest growing area of sales promotion Well over 120 billion coupons were established by manufacturers in 1982 according to the Nielsen Clearing House. This does not include all the coupons found in retailers' newspaper ads, which may equate to another thirty billion. Coupons are certificates that are placed in consumers' hands through door-to-door distribution or through direct mail, they can be part of a newspaper or magazine ad; they are in some packages, and on some packages. They can be in any amount ranging from two cents to a dollar or more. Most manufacturer's coupons are coded so that sorting and processing are easier.

Nevertheless, many retailers are less than enthusiastic about redeeming coupons. For one thing, the checkout process is slowed down. Time is required in sorting, handling, and counting. Then, the retailer must wait to be reimbursed. Certainly whether the two or three-cent handling allowance allowed by the manufacturer to the retailer is adequate is still debatable.

Combination offers link two products together for a price lower than if the products were purchased separately. Perhaps razor blade companies such as Gillette are most famous for this strategy when they offer free razor with the blades. Such promotions, as with all other sales promotions, are designed to give the consumer more value for the dollar on a short-term basis in order to boost sales. All such deals should be used only occasionally or the consumer will get the idea that the special price is the regular price.

Contests: Contests remain one of the most popular types of consumer promotions. Because of the increasing need of people to get "Something for nothing" along with some fortuitous legal developments chance contests have grown dramatically during the 1970s and 1980s. Although much of this popularity is due to a declining economy, the primary incentive was provided by the legal distinctions that determine what is or is not a lottery. The historic definition of a lottery shows it to be a promotion that involves the award of a *prize* on the basis of *chance* with a requirement of a *consideration* for entry. In a sales promotion program, the prize and the chance will be self-evident; the consideration, of course, is the box top or other purchase token asked for by the advertiser.

Because of the these legal factors, advertisers for many years employed contests of skill-eliminating the element of chance and thus removing the lottery stigma. The familiar 25-words-or-less contest and many other devices of the sort were common for years.

However, liberalization of some legal interpretations, including the ability to ask for a sales receipt as proof of purchase made the sweepstakes type of program feasible. *Consideration* had been effectively removed, and yet, the advertiser could ask for the consideration, with an "out", and get it in about 70 percent of the cases. Thus, contests of skill have largely yielded to contests of chance because of legal considerations as well as the skyrocketing costs of judging and processing contests of skill. Administering a skill contest costs about $ 350 per thousand entries. On the other hand, the cost of processing chance contests recently has ranged from $2.75 to $ 3.75 per thousand.

The relative growth of contests is quire complicated. Although there are not more recent figures, a total of $349 million was spent in 1967, with only $87.7 million projected for 1977. There is evidence that this trend has reversed itself in the 1980s. Some estimate that the increase has exceeded 300 percent since 1980.

There are many criticisms leveled at the use of contests. Most notably, critics are concerned with the many costs associated with designing an effective contest. Selecting appropriate prizes a particularly difficult problem. The prize must be attractive to the consumer, yet it must not overshadow the basic product sold by the sponsor. Often the relative attractiveness of cash, merchandise, or travel is a function of the particular market segment targeted. The media strategy employed to communicate the contest may also be complex and costly. Retailers may often be part of this process and may resent their participation. There are also critics who suggest that contests generate more ill will than goodwill. Losers may become opinion leaders against the company, particularly in light of the sandals associated with contests in the past. This brings up another criticism. Great care must be taken to meet the letter of the law in designing contests. For example, all prizes must be awarded. A final criticism concerns the effectiveness of contests. It is difficult to know that what level of sales increase is generated by the contest. More importantly, determining whether these customers are new or existing customers and whether they remain customers are important yet unanswered questions.

The arguments in favour of contests are also convincing. The primary argument in their favor is that contests generate mass interest and excitement-entries number in the millions-as well as a real enthusiasm among customers and employees. It also provides something new for the company to advertisers. After several months of creating me-too messages or desperately looking for a unique point to make, advertising people can let a contest take the burden off of them for awhile. Contest copy tends to write itself as long as it is supported by lots of enthusiasm and excitement in the background. Contents appeal to the consumer's desire to play, to compete, to win, to get something for nothing. The impact tends to be quite positive.

Rebates: Rebates first became popular in the mid-1970s and have remained popular. Simply states, a rebate is a refund of a fixed amount of money for a certain period of time. Rebates were initiated in 1974-1975 by automobile manufacturers in order to rid themselves of the huge inventories they had accumulated. They chose this approach rather than cutting prices because a rebate would not imply a lower price which the consumer might assume to be fixed. This strategy did move inventory but proved expensive to the manufacturers. Nevertheless, the strategy is still a primary element of the marketing program employed by the automobile industry.

Although the automobile industry has received the most notoreity over its rebate programs, such programs have been used by several types of industries. Cash rebates remain a viable sales promotion technique to build shopping traffic and to move certain products.

Premium offers: Although there are numerous definitions of what a premium is, suffice it to say that a premium is a tangible reward received for performing a particular act, usually purchasing a product. The premium can be considered something extra which makes the purchase of the product more appealing. The premium may be free, if not, the amount the consumer must pay is well below market prices. Premiums may be used to attract customers to a particular store, to buy a particular product, or to stimulate the purchase of larger amounts of a product. Thus, getting an extra amount of product is a premium, as is the prize in a Cracker Jack box, a free glass with Duz detergent, or a free atlas with the purchase of All state insurance.

The history of the premium is dotted with circus or stunt techniques. B.T. Babbitt, the originator of commercial premium promotion, ballyhooed his offer of lithographed pictures with a Barnum Bandwagon that traveled about the country, a fitting symbol of early premium use. Also, contributing to a scornful attitude of business in general toward consumer premiums was the fact that the term premium goods for decades meant just one thing-inferior merchandise, closeouts of off-standard items, and the cheapest of imports. Conservative business people turned pale at the very thought of indulging in such forms of promotion. Even many who came to use it through competitive pressure were a bit ashamed of the fact.

The decade beginning in 1946 was both a comeback road and an experimental period for the premium merchandiser. Programs dormant through the war were revived, with modification. Both new and old users conceived and tested new ways of applying had long looked with disfavor on premiums, began to study the question, to conduct research into premium methods and to recommend incentive plans to their clients. In short, premium merchandising at last was outgrowing the carnival air which had long surrounded it. A premium offer moved closer to the status of a measurable selling technique and became a fitting subject for through study by advertisers.

Perhaps the best way to discuss premiums is in respect to two general categories; direct premiums and mail premiums.

Direct premiums are incentives that provide immediate consumer action and give on-the-spot action in return. There is no confusion about money, mailing, clipping, chance, packaging, saving things, or tearing off box tops. Best of all, there is no waiting. Several generations ago direct premiums included small gifts from a storekeeper, free prints, books, or even the baker's dozen. By definition, a direct premium is usually considered to be one given free with the purchase at the time of the purchase.

Direct premiums are strong today in many fields-food, financial, institutions, toiletries, publishing, apparel, office supplies, and even the oil business; in this last instance, premiums slacked off in the mid-1970s, although they remain a significant factor. The stand out newcomer of the 1970s, is the fast-food restaurant business. In the separate direct premium gave way to a boom of factory-packs, and these have yielded a bit to the supermarkets frantic price cutting during the 1970s and 1980s, resulting in some cutback of manufacturer spending for any promotion involving merchandise at the point of sale. Much of the money has been diverted to discount couponing.

Four basic variations exist that qualify as direct premiums.

1. Incentives given separately at the time of a product purchase-the truly direct premium.

2. In-packs-interested into the product package at the factory as a plus to the consumer.
3. On-packs-another form of factory-pack that rides outside the package, firmly affixed to it by a paper or plastic band, sleeve, or other device.
4. Container premiums-which reverse the idea of the in-pack putting the product inside the premium instead of vice versa.

Direct premiums of the first variety had been the most common in grocery sales until the 1960s, when the mail premium appeared. The mail premium is considered a self-liquidator as enough is charged for the premium that it pays for itself. The last three variations were not widely used until recently. Then, they came as a sort of reaction from the overuse of self-liquidators, when many users sought a compromise between the cumbersome separate premium and the slow self-liquidator.

In 1975, the ten leading industries in use of direct premiums, with the factory-pack portion of their expenditures shown in parentheses, are listed below.

Food	$124,557,000
Banks, savings & loans	46,917,000
Petroleum products	25,533,000
Detergents, cleansers	16,908,000
Publishers, printers	14,677,000

Office equipment	11,722,000
Apparel	10,294,000
Feed, fertilizers	9,857,000
Building materials	6,937,000
Automobiles, trucks	6,544,000
Total	$271,946,000
Total	$479,043,000

These expenditure figures represent a relatively depressed level of promotion, with factory-packs down 15.3 percent from the previous years and other direct premiums off an estimated 16.6 percent.

Three other versions of the direct premium are; traffic-builders, door-openers, and referral premiums. Traffic-builder is a title given to many forms of promotions that holdout hope of bringing people into retail stores-under many guises from supermarket continuity promotions to loss leaders. But the true traffic-builder premium is none of these-it is, simply, an incentive to bring a prospect to one's place of business.

Where the traffic-builder tries to get doors opened from the outside, what we call a door opener aims at having them opened from the inside by consumers in their homes or business people in their officers. By far the most obvious user of door openers is the direct selling fields, in which door-opening favors are a staple device to get consumer's attention. Their use is a subtle foot-in-the-door on house-to-house canvassing-and sometimes a clincher in telephoning for an appointment. In addition, door-openers serve similar purposes in many other industries- wherever the ultimate sales effort must be made in the prospect's home or office. A copier manufacturer offers a desk item or a silver dollar or some other desirable item to the executive who agrees to hold still for an office demonstration.

The final category of premiums is based on referrals provided by the receiver. Many people believe that the best advertising is a satisfied customer. The use-the-user plan, as it used to be called, helps sellers in many fields to get sales leads from satisfied customers and to reward the present users with a premium for their assistance.

In its simplest form, the plan works this way. You have sold your product to Mrs.Consumer. She likes it. You ask her for the names of one or more friends who have seen the product and might be prospects to buy. You offer her an attractive incentive if any of the friends or neighbors buys. There are four basic variations.

1. Major appliance dealers salespeople may go into the customer's home, get names, and follow through in person with the prospects.
2. Many fraternal insurance associations and other member-ship organizations offer several different premiums to those who bring in their friends.
3. Direct sellers may ask customers for permission to use their names with friends and neighbors.

4. Party-plan operators, who repay hostesses with incentive also use them to book new parties. That is, the hostess whose guest agrees to hold a party of her own is usually rewarded with a premium in addition to those earned by sales at her party.

The self-liquidator is the primary type of mail premium and was invented during the 1930s as a result of commercial radio and the Depression. The Depression was a time of enforced thrift; savings measured in pennies on household necessities or minor luxuries were important to the average consumer. And, since promotion budgets were often tight, the idea of giving a premium that did not cost the advertiser anything was most attractive. The self-liquidator was the answer, though it was not so called for a number of years.

The principle is simple. You can give a much more valuable incentive and give it quickly, if the consumer is asked to pay a part of the cost in cash, along with a proof of purchase. The ideas of liquidating the total cost which eventually gave the method its present name was not a factor at first. Asking for any money seemed daring enough.

It was a short step for advertisers to ask for a little more money to make up the total cost of the incentive and to find that consumers still flocked to respond even when the once-free offer was reduced to a we'll-get-it-for-you-wholesale basis. Before long, the cash asked of consumers not only covered the wholesaler price of the premium, but also the total in-the-mail cost including packaging, mail handling, postage, insurance, and so on. Thus, the mail premium, in the truest sense, is nothing more than the advantage of the manufacturer's wholesale purchasing power.

Its advantages include the fact that each sampled consumer voluntarily goes into a retail store, picks up the product from a shelf, buys it at the regular price, and gets the full regular size. In addition, if you consider other psychological reaction, the customer is more likely to feel appreciation for the premium she receives than self-satisfaction at having "taken" the manufacturer by getting the product at a cut price.

As might be expected the food industry, is by far the largest single user of the self-liquidator. Other heavy users of mail-in-promotions are detergents and cleaners, toiletries, and beer, ale, and soft drinks. The ability of the liquidator to get displays used in the supermarket makes it highly attractive in that field. For example, Star-Kist Foods offered the consumer three choices in obtaining a Morris t-shirt. The consumer could get the t-shirt free for thirty cat food labels; pay $2.75 plus ten labels; or pay $5 and no labels. Newport cigarette offered a pocket camera for $10.95. A knee-length beach/sleep cover-up for $3.95. And an insulated cooler for $7.95-plus two bottom flaps from Newport packages in each case. At $15.95, Scott paper featured an outdoor grill. Van Camp's barbeque tool set went for $8.95; and the lowest-priced offering was a badminton set from Planters Peanuts for $7.95.

Of course, the mail premium area receiving the most publicity over the last two decades, are premimums offered to children. Actually, the tremendous increase in premium offers for kids came only with the development of the self-liquidator technique. As might be expected, the breakfast food people who are so prominent today as users of juvenile premiums were the pioneers a generation ago when it all started. In 1957, the big three in the cereal business spent between $5 million and $8 million vearlwon in-packs of very small cost, a penny or two a unit. Informal conversations among them led to a resolve to drop premiums in cereal boxes and to concentrate more on self-liquidators. This area is still controversial and the various promoters have attempted to provide meaningtul and safe premiums that are underthe $ 3 price category.

Trading stamps "The trading stamp system is the meanest, most individuious and by all odds the most contemptible fraud ever per petuated upon honest trade." This is a quote from a pamphlet entitled, Anti-Stamper. Story of the Trading Stamp Swindle, published by the Anti-Stamper Association in 1904. This anti-stamp attitude continued until the late 1950s when three out of four supermarkets gave trading stamps to their customers." At first, stamps were considered to be a merchandising tool of small retailers, enabling them to compete more effectively with chains.

However, this changed when the supermarkets became the nucleus of the trading stamp industry.

The boom of the 1950s ballooned the stamp industry from a handful of companies to more than 250 frims. By the late 1970s, their number had dropped back to about 40 to 50 firms issuing stamps through franchised retailers and redeeming their stamps for filled saver books. the customer usually gets one stamp for every dime spent in a participating store. A book is worth around $2.50 to $3.50 retail, and merchandise generally costs the stamp company from $1.25 to $1.75 a book. For the retailer, the entire packaged service-stamps, collection books, catalogues, redemption service and merchandise, and stamp-company advertising and promotion costs from 2 to 2 1/2 percent of sales volume.

The strength of a stamp program for individual retailers depends largely upon what they add to the plan to make it distinctive. One common criticism of stamps, as compared with other forms of incentive merchandising is that they tend to stagnate the creative process. But the good merchandiser beats this problem by using the stamp plan simply as a base from which to start a creative promotional program.

Trading stamps had enough troubles with the stamp-dropping, discounting supermarkets, but they were dealt a severe blow by the oil crisis of 1973 which almost instantly killed the rather large segment of stamp business done thrugh service stations. But the major weakness of the trading stamp program left over from the 1950s and 1960s was the sheer magniude of stamp usage. The field reached a level of a saturation that took away the competitive advantage that stamps were supposed to yield to their users. Particularly in the supermarket business where profits on sales were measured at 1 percent or less, spending 2 percent of sales for stamps measured at 1 percent or less, spending 2 percent of slaes for stamps was obviously unrealistic if the stamp plan did not yield the increased volume planned (i.e., 15 to 20 percent).

The independent stamp company as a service organization has several distinct responsibilities. Naturally, it must first have stamps of an exclusive design printed for issuance to the retailer customers as well as collection books, catalogues and display materials to go with them. Usually, too, it does a reasonable amount of advertising in local media to back up the retailers who issue the stamps. The service company maintains redemption centers for its customers, and, finally, has the buying responsibility for maintaining an adequate stock of several hundred attractive premium items that will not only gain initial consumer acceptance but deliver complete satisfaction. it must also maintain a substaintial cash reeserve for the redemption of stamps at any time.

Trading stamps may never return to the fever of the 1950s and 1960s. We may never again hear the many stories of women who run out of gas looking for stations that give their favorite stamps. Nevertheless, as one significant incentive tool among many, the trading stamp still has much work to do for many types of retail business.

Consumer sampling: One of the keys to success for many marketers is getting the physical product or service into the hands of the consumer. In some cases, particularly if the product is new or is not a markt leader, an effective strategy is to give the product to the consumer, either free or for a small fee. Because of the extremely high costs of sampling consumers in this manner, great care must be taken in employing this technique. A primary criteria is using sampling when you have a product that virtually sells itself. That is, the product must possess benefits or features that are easily discerned by the consumer. Another factor to consider is whether to provide the product free or to include a nominal charge. There are arguments for and against both. Obviously, giving the product away guaranties that the target market you wish to reach is sampled. On the other hand, this guarantee does not include a certainty that the product will actually be used. Many such products are not normal size, and the consumer has little remorse in discarding it or putting it away for future use. In addition, some consumers view products that cost nothing as being worth that amount. However, the norminal fee helps defray the costs of this promotional technique. Any charge, of course, works against the basic idea of sampling and may help defeat the sampling operation.

Products that are sampled tend to be low in price and have high turnover. It is important to give the consumer enough of the product so that the consumer can accurately judge its quality. More expensive products such as perfume, wines, and gourmet foods may also be sampled selectively with certain target markets. Even service products can be effectively sampled. For example, health clubs have been successful in attracting members by sending out coupons to a select group of people offering a free visit to the club.

There are several ways of distribuing the samples to the consumers. The most popular is through the mail. However, the tremendous increase in postage costs, combined with packaging and bundling requirements makes this method increasingly less attractive. An alternative is to use organizations that specialize in door-to-door distribution. This approach is particularly attractive with bulky items or in areas where reputable distribution organizations exist. This approach can also allow for a selective sampling technique, in that certain neighborhoods, dwellings, and even people can be selected. Also, these firms can vary their service from simply hanging a product on every product on every doorknob to actually delivering the product.

A version of such a commercial firm is the Welcome Wagon. In this case, a hired hostess calls on newcomers to the community. After welcoming them and answering their questions, she leaves product samples or coupons good for sampls from noncompeting manufacturers or retailers.

Another distribution method is in conjunction with advertising. This may involve a coupon that the consumer can mail in for the product or an address that is mentioned in the body of an advertisement. A similar message may also be included within radio and television messages. The cost of this approach may be quite high given the high cost of advertising space and the low response rate.

Products can slo be sampled directly through the retailers. This simply involves either setting up a display unit near the product that allows easy access to that product or hiring a person who physically distributes the product to consumers as they pass by. This technique helps build goodwill for the retailer and is effective in reaching the right consumers. On the other hand, retailers often resent the inconvenience and require high payments in order to cooperate. This technique might also create conflict with other brnds sold by the retailer.

The final form of distribution deals with specialty types of sampling. For instance, several companies specialize in packing a group of samples together and delivering the packaging a group of samples together and delivering the package to a homogeneous consumer group such as nelyweds, new parents, students, or tourists. Such packages may be delivered at hospitals, hotels, or student centers. There has been particular interest recently in the college freshman. Evidence exists which shows that many important longterm product decisions are made during the seventeen to nineteen year old time period. Consequently, incoming freshmen are given packages of products or coupons that can be redeemed for products. Selecting the approapriate products is critical with this group.

The arguments supporting sampling as a viable sales promotion device are numerous. Most notably, since it is more and more difficult for marketers to get consumers to take notice of their products, sampling appears to assist in this difficult problem. Also, samples can be distributed in conjunction with other elements of the promotional mix, greatly improging the impact of the overall strategy. The job of the salesperson is made easier when the product is actually in the hands of the consumer. As a matter of fact, sampling may be the primary reson why a retailer would select one manufacturer's product over another. Finally consumers like samples, especially when there is no risk.

The criticisms of sampling are also real. There is serious concern over whether sampling costs are excessive when the overall results are considered. Part of this problem relates to the fact that measuring sampling effectiveness is difficult. Perhaps the most serious criticism relates to the inability of the marketer to ascertain whether the product is appropriate for sampling. Aslo, a product must be unique or a exceptional quality in order to convince the consumer to actually go out and purchase it. The final criticism revolves around the negative image created by samples. For many people, sample products are synonymous with junk mail and are resented by the reciplents.

Packaging: It is cler that in the case of amny products the average consumer has a low level of product and brand awareness. In these cases, combined with the increeased popularity of self-service marketing, the product package becomes the primary selling device. Clearly, this importance is substantiated by the fact that companies spend nearly $50 billion a year on the development, design, and manufacturing of packages.

In respect to the definition given to sales promotion earlier, packaging is relly a quasi-form of slaes promotion. That is, in a very general sense, the package is an immediate incentive in addition to the base product offered to the consumer. Although it may not be separated from the base product and, consequently, is the product, it nevertheless has enough characteristics common to the techniques discussed thus far to be classified as sales promotion.

Since the inception of modern packaging in the early 1900s, packaging has had two primary purposes. The first is to simply protect the product. The technology in this area has been phenomenal. Packaging exists now that has dramatically extended product shelf life, as well as keeping the product inside safe from damage. In some instances the package protects the consumer from the product. The functional aspect of the package also includes the needs of the reseller.

Packages should be easy to box, nove, and stack on the retailers shelves.

The second primary purpose of packaging is its ability to promote. In this regard, packaging can perform several promotional roles. It can attrct the customers' attention and encourage them to examine the product. Through verbal and nonverbal symbols, the package can inform potential buyers about the product's content, features, uses, advantages, and hazards. A firm can create desirable images and associations by using certain colors, designs, shapes, and textures in packages. Many cosmetics manufacturers, for example, create impressions of richness, luxury, and exclusiveness by using packages of certain colors and shapes. A package may perform a promotinal function also when it is designed to be safer or more convenient to use, if such characteristics help stimulate demand. And, if a marketer develops a pacakage that can be reused for other purposes, the package may also promote the product.

Regardless of the specific objectives to be achieved by a package, the marketer must be constanntly cognizant of the impact that a package may have in promoting the product. For instance, changing the package may have a devastating effect on slaes. Attempting to sell a male-related product in a package the appears too feminie, may not lnly lose sales but may also cause the product to be shelved in the wrong part of the store. A package should reflect the positioning strategy of the firm in all ways, from the color, to the directions, to the style of lettering.

Employee promotions

Although not nearly as extensive as consumer sales promotions, promotional efforts directed at the employees of the company have became an important element of the overall marketing program. Just as there is a need to motivate the consumer to purchase the product, there is an equal need to motivate employees to work harder, to be positive opinion leaders about the company. And to purchase the product. The same high level of satisfaction that is desired in a customer is also desired in employees.

There is one aspect of this promotional effort that does create some confusion. Many of the programs desinged to motivate employees are the responsibility of management-primarily the personnel department. This is particularly true with plant-based employees. For example, placing a suggestion box in a plant is a common method reported to make the employees feel as though they are part of the decision-making process. Althoug this strategy was initated by personnel, the publicity introducing it, the awards given for good suggestions, and so on, may be the input of the promotional manager. Thus, you are forewarned that in the case of some of these motivational tecniques, several areas of management may be involved.

Promotions are directed at two groups of employees-plant-based and slaespeople. Although this classification claerly does not include all possible employees, it does reflect a huge majority.

Plant-based employees: Plant-based employees include all employees that are not directly responsible for making sales. It includes janitiors, office workers, assembly line workers, middle managers, top managers, and so on. It is with this group in partiuclar that many of the motivational programs are mor management inspired and directed. Also, most of these programs tend to be highly customized to the needs of the company or employee.

Perhaps the most common program of this type might be titled the orientation or indoctrination program. It is usually provided to blue collar employees and to employees at the managerial level who are new in the job market. This program can range from a short speech by someone in the personnel department to a slide presentation, to a full-scale multimedia program. Regardless of the sophistication of the program, the content tends to be the same history of the firm, description of products and distribution networks, company rules and policies, and reasons for being proud to work for that particular company. Although there are no measures as to the effectiveness of these programs, management assumes that providing this information can only help.

Another type of program aimed at plant-based employees includes a whole series of efforts that put the employee in contact with the product in some advantageous manner. The most common of these is the company store. Although this may not acutally in volve a real sotre the crux of the incentive is to allow employees to purchase company products at a greatly reduced price. In the case of companies with a great many subsidiaries, this could mean a substantial savings for the employee.

For General Motors employees or those working for Airstream it would equate to several hundred dollars off on the purchase of their next automobile or travel trailer. Another program under this heading is to use employees as part of the product testing process. In some cases, this may even include advertising, packaging, and pricing. For example, may razor blade manufacturers encourage their male employees to shave at the plant every morning with some version of their product. Texas Instruments has market tested many of their learning aids products with the children of employees.

Another whole set of programs directed at plant-based employees, as well as salespeople, fall under the heading of *fringe benefits*. This includes hospitalization, life insurance, profits sharing, bonus systems, stock options, free uniforms, and free parking just to name a few. Although these programs tend to fall under the auspices of the personnel department, the promotion department can assist in designing material to present and explain the programs to employees. The support of many employees has been lost because they misunderstood the benefits they thought they were to receive.

The final set of programs might be labelled as company image or institutional promotion efforts. Research has shown that it is important for employees to be proud of the company for which they work. Consequently, many companies like Texaco, Philips, and Xerox spend a great deal of money on institutional advertising that attempts to portray the company as caring and concerned with the well-being of society. Although it is directed primarily at consumers, it can also have a positive impact on employees. It is reported that after Avis introduced the "We Try Harder" campaign for several years, the morale at Hertz was so bad the Hertz came out with a set of commercials to change their image as the "bully" of the industry. Other forms of promotion that have been employed are company sponsorship, exhibits, and public service.

Salespeople: Sales promotion activities directed at the sales force is classified in two ways. The first set of activities deals with programs that better prepare salespeople to do their job. This includes sales manuals, training programs, and sales presentations as well as supportive materials such as films, slides presentations as well as supportive materials such as films, slides, and other visual aids. The second set of activities are concerned with promotional efforts or incentive that will motivate salespeople work harder. The types of incentive employed has greatly expanded during the last decade.

Training, the first set of activities, tends, to be closely related to the job of the sales manager and will be covered in greater detail in the chapter on personal selling. However, in some firms, the sales promotion staff actually has the responsibility of training and equipping the sales force. They are often involved in designing the actual presentation employed by the sales force. This might include the sales manual, product catalogues, visual aids, photographs, and other materials. Of course, depending on the needs and orientation of th company, the sales promotion staff might be involved in a small part of this effort or not at all.

Probably one of the most common and popular activities under this heading is the sales meting. These meetings can take place at the local level or internationally, although national meetings are the norm. Depending upon the company and its objectives, the meeting will be dome combination of business and pleasure. Often times, local and regional meetings will be very business-oriented and the national meetings will be primarily educational and social. Although the social elements are important and can be and effective from of motivation, the training and educational elements tend to be more meaningful.

Since companies spend millions of dollars on training and education, it is important that these meetings are planned and executed properly. They should be designee to meet the particular objectives of the group attending. For relatively new salespeople, these meetings might involve the emphasis might be on motivation or morale. In either case, the meeting must be customized to the audience and every detail should be settled before the meeting begins. It is important that the participants understand the extent to which each meeting is to be business versus pleasure.

Another part of the training-related process developed for the sales force is *supportive materials*. This tends to be illustrative materials that either provide information to the salesperson or materials that can be used directly in the sales presentation . In the case of technical companies with extensive product lines the sales manual might be several books. It usually contains product descriptions, price, manufacturing processes, delivery times, product application,s and suggested sales techniques to name but a few. The sales manual is as important to the salesperson as a playbook is to a professional football player. Because much of the information is confidential and the salesperson may make extensive notes within it, it is guarded closely. Often, the sales promotion staff has a large part in the design of this manual.

Sales portfolios and product models are devices that are used in conjunction with the sales presentation. The portfolio can take many forms; a flip chart, a ring binder, slides, photographs, transparencies, and so on. It is coordinated with the verbal presentation to illustrate and highlight certain parts of the presentation. The models serve the same purpose, depending upon the need. Some products demonstrate very well, others do not. A prototype or scale model might work well for small equipment, but look like a ridiculous toy for a three-story overhead crane. In the latter case slides or a movie might be substituted, or even more common, the prospect would be taken to where the product is installed and operating. Here again, sales promotion expertise is employed to develop and design the appropriate materials.

There are also materials that the sales force receives on a some what regular basis. One such example is the house organ. Also known as the company newsletter, newspaper, or magazine, its purpose is to relay company programs, policies, new products, meetings, awards, and retirements to the personnel. Larger companies may also develop special bulletins may highlight certain products, meetings, or people. In any case, these types of communications can be helpful in making the salesperson feel informed and in creating higher morale and motivation for the entire sales force.

Developing incentive programs for the sale force is very much the domain of the sales promotion department. Sales incentives have been the fastest growing segment of the incentive field for twenty years and now also represent the largest single segment at an annual rate of expenditure estimated at about $1.29 billion for 1977. It is not difficult to understand the popularity of this device for improving sales performance. The sales force of any company represents a more or less captive audience-measurable and capable of being reached most readily. This is the most direct point at which one can apply stimulus to add profitable volume.

Although the prizes or awards given to a salesperson as part of the incentive program are very important, they are only a part of the incentive program. There are several other consideration in this process. The first step is to determine the objective program, whatever its specific orientation to sales goals, is to get a little more sales effort from everyone in the organization. To do this, the incentives must obviously be keyed to each participant's individual past performance and present potential. This suggests, of course, the setting of quotas as a basis for awarding incentives, of course, the setting of quotas as to basis for awarding incentives, and a majority of sales incentive campaigns do indeed base awards on quotas. In fact, the wisdom and equity of quotas may very well determine the success of the entire program. While specific objectives are as individual as the sales manager's name, common objectives are to:

introduce a product to a new distribution area,

reduce selling costs.

improve working habits,

offset competitive promotions and

increase total sales volume.

Another value of defining objectives lies in the fact that it forces a closer examination of just how the incentive campaign is going to arrive at the objective. This is the second step in the process-to communicate clearly to members of the sales force precisely what they are expected to achieve and how they are to achieve it. This begins by specifying the basis of awards. Four broad methods are used to provide award credits to salespeople.

1. A fixed number of awards are given to the top producers in terms of total volume
2. Awards are tied to unit sales on an absolute basis.
3. A fixed number of awards are given to those performing best in relation to their individual quota.
4. A quota is set individually for each salesperson, and awards are based on the percentage of quota performance.

A third stop in designing an incentive program is deciding just which members of the sales force should participate. In some cases, all salespeople may be the obvious answer. But if there are several categories of salespeople, divided by product line, by type of account, or in some other manner, it may be appropriate to limit the campaign to one or to groups or to provide different goals and rules for different classes of sales personnel.

The fourth step involves several time decisions. Three time factors are important: the specific break time of the promotion, the duration of the campaign, and the planning lead time allowed to prepare for the push. The promotion break date has to be dictated by marketing decisions. For example, if the sales incentive program backs a trade or consumer promotion or if a new product is being introduced, these factors will determine when the campaign begins. How long to run the programs is influenced by the user's product distribution, type of salespeople, program objective, and the executives' experience or feeling as to what works best for their particular organization. The average length is slightly over eighteen weeks. The other aspect of incentive timing is how much time is required for advance planning. In recent surveys, the average lead time has fluctuated quite a bit, between twelve and twenty weeks. During times of economic uncertainty this time frame is substantially reduced.

Deciding upon the type of awards and prize structure is the fifth step in the incentive planning process. This decision is closely interrelated with other factors such as budget, length of campaign, theme, and the nature of the salespeople ad individuals, to understand their income level, social and economic status, personal interests and tastes, and anything else that will help plan a successful prize selection.

Initially, the decision begins with a choice between offering travel, merchandise, or a combination of the two. Travel has come to be the glamour incentive award in recent years, and users will probably wish to consider it if they are planning a relatively long-term promotion with a budget that can be tailored to offer trips to a fair number of winners at the top-with merchandise awards for lower qualifiers. In 1977, the average cost of trips awarded was $1009 and the average cost on merchandise was $175.

In locking at the specific types of merchandise utilized in sales incentive programs, there are no particular rules except the obvious ones of fitting types of items to the people involved and of matching budget allocations. But it may be useful to see what merchandise is selected by large numbers of salespeople when they are given free choice from a catalogue of thousands of items. Table 13.3 provides a breakdown of the 1976 redemptions provided by the MacDonald Incentive Company. Besides merchandise and travel, there are two other forms, of prizes used- cash an honor awards. Cash has several drawbacks associated with it. It has motivational; power to the same degree as the salary or commission income of the salesperson, but no special stimulus or recognition value. There are also practical arguments against cash awards. First, cash will buy from a third to twice as much when put into merchandise form. Also, awards offered to salespeople are usually in a class the recipients look on as luxuries. Thus, these awards are special, while recipients look on a luxuries. thus, these awards are special, while the cash may not be. However, during economic down times, cash awards may gain in appeal.

Honor awards appear to be a more positive form of reinforcement. They provide recognition in its purest from, although they usually lack the intrinsic value of tangible awards. A weakness in the use of honor awards alone is that they must be few in number if the honor if to have real meaning, thus they cannot bring broad participation in the sales force. As a resuslt, honor awards may often be an ideal recognition element to add to a merchandise or travel incentive program, enhancing the psychological effects of winning at small additional cost to the company.

The sixth and final step in developing a sales incentive program is selecting a theme. Confronted with an important objective, a realistic quota, workable rules and attractive awards, one would think that the average salesperson would be ready to work their tail off for the ABC Corporation. However, it doesn't work that way. The salespeople may know all the right answers as to what they should do and how; they may have clear view of their own self interest in the program, and they may still just stand there. They have to be sold, and sold had, at every throughout the campaign. Their imaginations have to be sparked and their enthusiasm fixed up.

All the things a sales manager and promotion manager do to promote a campaign stem from one or more words that are called a theme. The theme of a sale incentive program is much the same as any other theme, except it may appear a bit more outlandish in some cases. A theme of some sort is necessary to provide a frame for the whole picture of the incentive program, to give unity to the promotional materials, and to add a little extra fun. Popular themes have been related to games or sports, travel, company honor club, and sales objective tie-ins to name but a few.

Distributor or dealer promotions

Everybody knows what a middleman or dealer is, but it's hard to find agreement on how to move this person to desired action. A dealer to generalize a bit is someone with a very hard head full of gross margin figures, with a store full of absolutely priceless shelf space, and with very little imagination when it comes to merchandising a manufacturer's product. While the stereotype may be somewhat overdrawn, it is still basically true that in most fields the state of dealer relationships is a source of major frustration. The retailer's perfectly good arithmetic tells him to get the best dollar movement out of every square foot. The manufacturer is certain he had an appealing formula, if the dealer will only push it. Bringing the two points of view closer together is partially the responsibility of sales promotion.

There are a great many promotional devices available to the manufacturer that hopefully will convince or motivate middlemen to engage in certain activities. The appropriate devices to employ depended on a myriad of factors such as type of middleman, services and so on. These promotional devices include:

Point-of-purchase displays,
Contests,
Trade shows,
Sales meetings.
Push money,
Dealer Loaders.
and Trade Deals.

Point-of-purchase display: Point-of-purchase displays are provided free by the manufacturer to the retailer in order to promote a particular brand or group of products. The forms POP displays take is really a function of the industry but can include special racks, display cartons, banners, signs, price cards, and mechanical product dispensers. In an industry such as the grocery field where a consumer spends about three-tenths of a second viewing a particular product, anything that can give a product greater visibility is valuable. This is even more important when evidence suggests that a large percentage of the consumers' choices are actually made in the retail store. And since most retailing is totally or partially self-service, displays play a big role in the decision-making process.

However, it is one thing for manufacturers to know POP displays are good for them, but quite another to convince retailers that they will benefit as well. Unfortunately, this is not always accomplished, as judged by a recent estimate is never used by retailers probably the most effective incentive for a middleman to use a POP is for the manufacturer to take great care in planning and designing every detail of the display. If a retailer is willing to use your display there must be a high probability that it will generate greater sales for the retailer. It is important that the theme shown on the POP material is coordinated with the theme used in advertisements and by salespeople. In addition, the display should be designed with the physical elements of the retailer in mind. Since shelf space is at such a premium, the display should not waste it. Many of the most successful supermarket displays are end-of-the -aisle structures that take up no self space. The display should also be well-designed. Structurally, it should be constructed of quality materials so tha tit is sturdy, will not fall apart, and can be easily assembled and unassembled. Aesthetically, the display should use colors, pictures, and shapes that are attractive and that harmonize with the general theme of the store. Finally, one of the most successful ways of promoting POP materials is through a professional, well-planned presentation. In the case of Proctor and Gamble, this involves many hours of preparation which would include supportive statistics, examples of the POP, a discussion of the promotional strategy, and good selling techniques.

Contests: As was the case in motivating salespeople, contests can also be developed to motivative middlemen. Thus, much of the criteria described earlier applies equally as well with channel members, The prize tend to be the same, and there is often a need to customize the program for the particular reseller group one is trying to motivative. Typically, the prize is awarded to the organization or person who exceeds quota by the largest percentage.

Great care is necessary in designing contests. Although there is a need to involve as many people as possible in a contest, the rewards offered may be so stimulating that the possible winners might engage in activities that are detrimental to their companies. Retail salesclerks have been known to push the product of the contest company to he total exclusion of competing brands. These practices can cause serious conflict between channel members. Also, the length and quality of contests need to be carefully governed. Contests are only effective if they take place periodically. This notion of "Something special" should also be displayed in the manner in which the contest is promoted and organized and in which the prize are awarded. Contests can provide short-term benefits and can help improve the relationship between the manufacturer and other middlemen if conducted properly.

Trade shows: Thousands of manufacturers of consumer and industrial products display their wares at trade shows. For many types of businesses, trade shows provide the major opportunity to actually write orders for their products. For others, it allows them to demonstrate their products, provide information, answer questiaons, and to be compared directly with their competitors.

In turn, trade shows allow manufacturers to gather a great deal of information about their competition. Since all the companies are attempting to provide a clear picture of their own products to potential customers, this same informations is available to competitors. Consequently, quality, features, prices, and technology can be easily compared.

The motivational aspects of trade shows

cannot be underestimated. The booths ae usually staffed by the manufacturer's top salespeople. The trade show bring these salespeople into direct contact with top executives representing various middle agents. The salesperson can meet these people, introduce the product, demonstrate, it, field questions, gather information, and estanlish future contacts. the social aspects of trade shows is also important, The atmosphere tends to be relaxed. A great many free products are distributed. Parties are sponsored by most manufacturers. Unfortunately, this element of trade shows can get out of hand, and sales are garnished by the company that spends the most money on the most outrageous party.

Although the trade shows require a bit less formal than the normal selling situation, it does not mean that any less care should go into its planning. Companies spend more than $7 billion annually on trade shows, and the success for the entire year may hinge on how well a company performs at the trade shows. For many companies, all their panning efforts and much of their marketing budget and efforts are directed at the trade show.

Sales meetings: Somewhat related trade meetings, but not nearly as elaborate, are sales meetings sponsored by manufacturers or wholesalers. Usually, these meetings are conducted at the regional level and are directed by sales managers and their field force. In some instances, a major marketing officer from corporate headquarters may direct the proceedings. The purposes for these meetings are quite varied. Oftentimes, they occur just prior to the buying season and are used to motivate middle agents, to explain various aspects of the product or the promotional campaign, or simply to answer questions.

Besides annual or semi-annual meetings, there are also periodic meetings that may be called for a whose set of additional reasons. A common set of reasons revolve around the need to stimulate through contests or facts and figures, to discuss problems, and to announce new products. Sales training is also a major part of these meetings. However, a company mist be careful anytime it takes employees away from their job. In many cases, special incentives must be offered just to guarantee attendance.

Push money: Although he term *push money* has acquired a negative, almost illegal interpretation, it is a common technique used by many manufacturers. It simply means that for a given period of time, a manufacturer will pay a retail salesperson a monetary bonus for every unit of product sold. for example, a manufacturer of refrigerators might pay a $30 bonus for model A, $25 for model B, and $20 for model C, between May I and September 1 . At the end of that period, the salesperson would send in evidence of these sales to the manufacturer and would receive a check in a few days.

As is the case in most of marketing, there are certain situations in which push money is more effective. Undoubtedly, it works much better when the salesclerk has an inherent responsibility for the sale of the product. Products that have to be demonstrated, explained, or have a high unit cost would be nest. This strategy also requires the complete cooperation of the retailer. If retailers feel that push money would be had for morale or would cause a disproportionatc cmphasis on a particular brand, they will more than likely veto its use. There are also some ethical assumes related to push money that have not year been resolved. Still, the techniques can create a great deal of enthusiasm and motivation at the middle agent level and will continue to be used under the guidelines of the Federal Trade Commission.

Dealer loaders: A dealer loader is a premium that is given to a retailer by a manufacturer for buying a certain amount of product. Although there are several possible combinations, two types of dealer loaders are most common. The first is labeled *buying loaders* and are typically gifts given for buying a certain order size. The second is called *display loaders* which is essence is a display that is given to the retailer after it has been taken apart. For instance, General Electric any have a display containing several types of appliances as part of a special program. When the program is over, the retailer would receive all the appliance if he had purchased the specified order size

Both strategies can be successful in the right situation. Buying loaders are most often used as a door opener in order to get shelf space in a new retail outlet, or when an exceptionally large amount of product must be sold. Display loaders are used in conjunction with special promotions when it is important to get the point-of-purchase display into the store. The underlying motivation for both is to move large amounts or product in a short period of time.

Trade deals: Trade deals incorporate a whole series of strategies that have one common these-to encourage middlemen to give your product special promotional effort that it would not normally receive. These promotional efforts can take the form of special displays, larger than usual amounts being purchased, superior store locations, or just greater promotional effort. In return retailers receive special allowances, discounts, goods, or cash.

The money spent on trade deals is substantial, and in many industries, such as groceries, it is a fundamental way of doing business. As such, trade deals are expected in many business and may provide the primary incentive in-receiving retail support. In addition, these programs are flexible and can be changed from day-to-day or even more frequently if necessary. The largest problem is making sure that everyone in the organization is aware of these frequent changes. There are many examples of companies that created bad will or lost customers because not all the parties processing the sales order were aware of these changes. Finally, trade deals can be combines with other promotional strategies that provide an irresistible package for a particular middleman.

The negative aspects of trade are also quite real. The most serious has already been alluded to earlier . In many industries trade deals are expected, and a manufacturer who did not offer such incentives would be doomed to failure. Obviously, these deals can get out of hand quite easily. In some situation, where the retailer may dominate the channel, manufacturers may be played against one another until some have reduced their profit levels to and untenable point. There are able the problems of retailers either not passing the discount on to the consumer or not meeting their end of the agreement. In the former instance, the program developed by the manufacturer may revolve around a lower price. If the retailer does not cooperate, the manufacturer is put into a disadvantageous position. The latter problem exists because it is so difficult to monitor the many retail outlets involved in the promotion. Even if retailers are suspected of pocketing allowance money, there is a great risk in confronting them with the fact.

There are two general types of trade deals, The first type is referred to as *buying allowances* and includes situations whereby a manufacturer pays a middleman a certain amount of money if a certain amount of product is purchased during a certain time period . With this strategy, meeting the specifications of the deal is all that is required of the retailer. The payment may be given in the form of a check form the manufacturer or a reduction in the face value of an invoice.

The *count and recount* techniques is one approach used as part of the buying allowance. This is the offer of a certain amount of only for each unit of product moved out of a wholesaler's or retailer's warehouse during a specified time period. The title comes from the fact that the local sales representative will take account of merchandise on hand at the beginning of the period and a final recount at the end of the time period. Thanks to the computer, this counting process can be greatly simplified.

A *buy-back allowance* is another type of buying allowance. This allowance immediately follows another type of trade deal and offers a specified amount of money for new purchases of the product base upon the quantity of purchases made on the first deal. Its purpose is to motivate repurchase of a product immediately after another trade deal on the product has served to deplete warehouse stock. For example, Proctor & Gamble might offer $1.50 off the price of a case of Head and Shoulders on a count-recount deal between July 1 thru July 31 and then offers $1.00 per case on a buy-back allowance from August 1 thru August 31. The amount allowed on the buy-back cannot exceed the amount bought on the count-recount deal.

The final type of buying allowance is referred to as *free goods* allowance. This is the offer of a certain amount of product to wholesalers or retailers at no cost but based upon the buying of a stated amount of the same or another product of the manufacturer. The middle agent is given free merchandise instead of money. Simply illustrated, manufacturer might offer a retailer one free case of merchandise for every twenty purchased.

The second category of trade deals retails to *advertising and display allowances*. An *advertising allowance* is a common technique employed primarily in the consumer products area. In this situation, the manufacturer pays the wholesaler or retailer a certain amount of money for advertising the manufacturer's product. The money can only be used to purchase advertising, although policing this process may prove difficult. Many manufacturer's will require some evidence of performance on order to assure themselves of proper behavior. Nevertheless, middlemen may view this as a type of personal bonus and engage in devious behavior such as billing the manufacturer at the much higher national rate rather than the local rate. Several types of criteria can be used to determine the amount of the allowance, from a flat dollar amount to a percentage of gross purchase during a specified time period. Closely related to an advertising allowance is *cooperative advertising*. This is a contractual arrangement between the manufacturer and the middle agents whereby the manufacture agrees to pay a part or all of the advertising expenses incurred by the middleman in advertising the manufacturer's product. The deal is usually restricted to newspaper, radio, or television advertising. Here again, because of a few dishonest middlemen, manufacturers normally do not pay for the advertising until they get some verification from the medium or a copy, of the advertisement.

Another form of display or advertising allowance is a *dealer listing.* In this instance, a manufacturer may be announcing a new product or running a special promotion. As part of a regional or national campaign the manufacturer will provide space on the advertisement to list all the retailers at which the product may be purchased. This technique not only generates traffic for the retailer but also makes the retailer feel like he is receiving a direct benefit by the manufacturer. There is also a certain prestige involved when a local retailer has his name associated with a national advertisement.

A *display allowance* is the final form of promotional allowance. Retailers are shown many displays by manufacturers every week. Some manufacturers will pay retailers to select their display. This payment can be in the form of cash or goods. Retailers must furnish written certification of compliance with the terms of the contract before they are paid. Again, because so many manufacturers offer this allowance, retailers tend to select display that yield high- volume and high profits, as well as being easy to assemble.

Sales promotion has become a primary part of the promotional strategy rather than a secondary element of promotion that is considered after the advertising is designed and paid for, Stated simply, it is that something extra that is offered to the consumer. This chapter discussed the importance of sales promotion, its unique characteristics, and the reasons for its continued growth.

The bulk of the chapter outlined sales promotion in respect to its three primary target markets; consumers, employees, and distributors. Each area was then dealt with in terms of the specific sales promotion techniques. In the case of consumer sales promotion, price deals, contests, rebates, premium offers, trading stamps, consumer sampling, and packaging were discussed. Employee sales promotions included plant-based programs and sales force programs. For the distributors, point-of-purchase materials, contests, trade shows, push money, and so forth were considered.

3 Multinational Sales Management and Foreign Sales Promotion

Personal selling, sales promotion, and public relations are all devices of a company's total promotional scheme, but each one has certain characteristics that assign it a unique role. When a company begins selling in export markets, or switches from export selling to international marketing, or launches a new product line or service in a new foreign market, or takes an established line of products into a new country or region, it invariably has more promotion tasks to undertake than funds available. In other words, marketers' aspirations with respect to foreign marketing almost always exceed their ability or willingness to allocate funds. This chapter highlights the significance of different types of promotion and examines their relevance in different foreign situations. Unfortunately, no ready-made formulas are available to give priority to different forms of promotion. However, the discussion here identified considerations that may help in determining where to begin and how to begin.

Personnel and personal selling abroad

Sales personnel in international business can be classified in two ways, either by the task they perform or by their nationality. Principally, there are three categories of selling tasks: sales generation, sales support, and missionary work. Sales generation is the creative task of helping the customer to make a purchase decision. Sales support is concerned with after sales service. Missionary work is undertaken by a manufacturer's salespersons to stimulate demand to help the distributors. When classifying sales personnel by nationality, there are also three categories: expatriates, natives, and third country nationals. Expatriates are home country employees on deputation in the host country. For example, a G.E. sales manager from the United States assigned to launch the G.E. sales effort in Spain would be considered an expatriate. Natives are employees belonging to the host country. A Spanish national working for G.E. As a salesperson in Spain is a native. Third country nationals are employees transferred from one host country to another. For example, a French national transferred to Spain would be defined as a third country national.

For the most part, U.S. companies do not transfer selling personnel abroad. There are two reasons for this. First, selling requires deep familiarity with the local culture, which an expatriate cannot be expected to have, and second it is extremely expensive to assign expatriates to selling positions. Such reasons lead companies-

IBM as an example-to depend mainly on nationals for selling jobs. There are occasions, however, when companies may assign expatriates to work, usually for short periods, in the selling area. Such a practice is more commonly usually for short periods, in the selling area. Such a practice is more commonly followed in the marketing of big-ticket items. The expatriate who has a proven track record at home can be quite helpful in resolving difficult foreign situations, and/or in serving as a catalyst of the natives. For example, Otis Elvator has to assign a sales engineer from the home office to provide after sales service for its elevators in a large office complex in Singapore for a year. This became necessary because the native sales force had failed to ensure smooth functioning of its elevators. Likewise, NCR corporation uses expatriates to provide on-the-job training to natives. As a matter of fact; the company has a cadre of seasoned salespeople who travel from country to country assisting native salesforces in selling company's products. Many big-ticket items require selling directly from the home office, which usually involve expatriates. For example, Boeing bids for selling airliners to foreign airlines from its headquarters in Seattle. Its salespeople mainly expatriates, travel extensively worldwide to call on its customers. In 1983, Greece decided to rejuvenate its air force by buying 100 new fighter bombers. This amounted to over $3 billion worth of business, Greece's biggest-ever defense contract. A number of U.S aircraft companies and European companies sent sales personnel to Athens to make sales presentations and contacts.

The management of a native salesforce is a local matter to be handled according to business practices in the host country. From the viewpoint of parent corporations, therefore, the major concern is with expatriates and third country nationals. Foreign sales positions are demanding assignments that require long hours of hard work, perseverance, and self-sacrifice. Developing the long-term relationship necessary for successful selling in a foreign environment takes tremendous effort.

Expatriates

The recruitment, transport, and risks connected with sending expatriate sales people overseas are time consuming and expensive, ranging from two-and-a-half to three times the costs involved with an equivalent domestic salesperson. In addition, an MNC risks a loss of time and money if the salesperson fails to stay the length of the assignment. Productivity may suffer too if the person becomes a so-called brownout-someone who stays on the foreign assignment but becomes inefficient because either he or she or the family is unhappy. Also an expatriate's inefficient because either he or she or the family is unhappy. Also an expatriate's inefficient because either he or she or the family is unhappy. Also an expatriate's lack of knowledge or disregard for the host country's cultural practices may damage a company's reputation or cause the loss of a critical contract. Finally, the MNC should be concerned with the repatriation of expatriates in order to reassimilate them into the stream of domestic corporate activity without loss of efficiency.

In addition to using expatriates for sales positions overseas for limited periods, many companies place expatriates for sales positions overseas for limited periods, many companies place expatriates in foreign subsidiaries for reasons that may be hard to accept. A study by Gallbraith and Edstrom offers four reasons for using expatriates. While the study deals with foreign placement in general. It has equal application for the assignment of salespeople overseas. The reasons were (1) to fill a position, (2) to utilize managerial talent, (3) to give an executive international experience, and (4) to facilitate coordination and control with the parent company.

The first reason usually results from a technical position becoming vacant in a subsidiary located in a developing country, where the lack of technically qualified personnel motivates the move. One example is the recruitment of engineers for high-paying positions in the middle East. According to the study, this reason accounted for 60 to 70 percent of all transfers.

The second reason to use managerial talent, is explained by the authors as follows "a job opportunity and a promotable individual do not always occur in the same subsidiary." This situation complements the first. An absence of opportunity at home and a need overseas would encourage the transfer of a talented individual to a subsidiary outside the United States.

The third reason, to provide international

experience for executives, was cited by U.S. firms in the study as the second most important criterion for foreign assignment. This consideration, however, is not independent of the need to fill a position. If there are qualified local managers and the transfer occurs, then the probable reason is valuable international experience and exposure. Knowledge gained during the assignment would increase the firm's global perspective in relating to existing markets. Firsthand information is always preferable. This leads to the fourth reason, coordination and control, which is particularly crucial in situations where the firm is initiating large efforts to crack a local market, where the organization is implementing policy changes, or where the firm lacks confidence in developing countries.

It is quite logical to bring in expatriates for specific so-called fire-fighting assignments or for a developmental assignment, that is, to expose a promising executive to multinational experience. The problems occur when people are sent overseas for historical or egocentric or nationalistic reasons like: "But we've always had an expatriate do that job. No one can manage that operation except an American." Political maneuvering within a company can also cause problems, like sending an employee overseas to clear the way for another person to take up an emerging position. Retreading the path of least resistance-that is, the best solution is always to bring in an American whenever there is any problem-can be counterproductive.

In recent years, a new trend has been to assign employees at all levels from one host country to another. This trend has arisen for two reasons. One, in many countries of the world there is a surplus of workers, while other countries lack adequate work forces. For example, Saudi Arabia's population is about 6 million people. If a company is developing fast, it may need a large sales force. It may find it difficult to find suitable Saudis to fill sales positions. Saudi Arabia is, therefore, forced into accepting salespeople from other developing countries, like Pakistan, India, or South Korea. Too, a company often needs a salesperson with certain requisite experience for a subsidiary. Looking around, the company discovers the most appropriate person for the job is a third country national.

Thread country individuals face unique organizational problem. For example, third country employees naturally want to know to which organization, the parent corporation or the host country company, they belong in regard to promotion and benefits and their feeling of identity. To manager third country employees effectively, both headquarters and host country management should study their special problems. An appreciation of their needs enhances performance for the benefits of the corporation.

The following account illustrates how the transfer of third country employees sometimes leads to trouble. Although the episode concerns and executive, it is equally relevant for salespersons.

The scene is the West Coast headquarters of a worldwide high-technology company. It is late in the afternoon and an all-day conference involving the personnel director and the vice president of international operations is in progress.

What is the problem? The problem is Pierre. Who is Pierre? He is not just another militant employee off the assembly line. Pierre is a key executive, two levels from the top of the organization, and, heretofore, regarded as a comer headed for a key top-management position in the United States upon conclusion of his current assignment.

How did Pierre get in this fix? He was hired in Parts and managed the French subsidiary until it achieved significant market penetration in France. One day Pierre woke up ad found that the job had lost challenge. There was nowhere for him to go. He was a big fish in a small pond. About the same time, the company was beginning operations in Australia.

Problems faced by Third-Country Nationals

- *Blocked promotions.* The tendency of MNCs to reserve top positions at headquarters for parent country managers.
- *Transfer anxieties.* The third country manager anxieties caused by uncertainty about the timing of their next transfers, the countries to which they will be transferred, the positions to which they will be assigned, and the extent of managerial autonomy involved in their next assignments.

- *Income gaps*. The tendency of third country managers to feel deprived in terms of income in comparison to parent country managers, and the tendency of host country managers to feel deprived in comparison to third country managers.
- *Unfamiliarity and adaptability difficulties*: The natural tendency of newly arrived third country managers to make mistakes and their compulsion to cover them up.
- *Avoidance of long-range projects*: The tendency of third country managers to concentrate on short-range, nonrisk, and demonstration-type projects.
- *Inappropriate leadership style:* The tendency of third country managers to imitate the managerial style prevalent at headquarters.
- *Nonparticipative decision making and screening of information*: The tendency of third country managers to adopt a detached leadership style because of their perception of headquarters as their positive reference group.
- *Insufficient authority in industrial relations*: The tendency of MNCs to delegate insufficient authority to third country managers in top positions for dealing with critical industrial relations issues in their subsidiaries.
- *Lack of commitment of top ranking third country managers to the perpetuation of the host country organization*: The conviction of host country managers that third country managers are less

committed to the perpetuation of the host country organization and to the welfare of their host country subordinates.

Formulating policy guidelines.

The high rate of expatriate failure among U.S. multinations is a matter of great concern. It stems form several factors the family situation, lack of cross-cultural relational abilities, the short duration of overseas assignments, problems of repatriation, overemphasis on the technical competence criterion to the disregard of other important attributes such as relations abilities, and inadequate training for cross-cultural encounters.

Companies can no longer afford to transfer people from nation to nation without having an appropriate policy for a guide. Too many people and too much money are involved. While the common practice is to hire natives for sales positions, the number of short-term specific assignments for solving ad hoc problems is one the increase, which requires bringing in expatriates or third country nations. The policy should cover determination of the most appropriate nationality, the selection of the nonnative salesperson, plans for repatriation and reassignment, work assignments, and the development of native salespersons by the nonnative selected. In actuality, companies may not have a thoroughly articulated policy for expatriates and third country nationals that covers all these points. But increasingly companies attach importance to the problems that occur when people work in different cultures. As an example, Westinghouse Corporation has defined the following corporate procedure for assignment repatriation, and reassignment of international employees:

Background: The long-term interest of the Corporation is best served by limiting international assignments to those management and professional employees who have an established record of competence. International assignments can be a valuable supplement to the normal training and development programs for the high-potential employee.

Management and professional people with international experience are an invaluable corporate asset, and every effort should be made to assure that experience gained by employees through such assignments is retained and properly utilized.

Consequently, all organization units assigning personnel internationally should develop specific plans for the selection, assignment, and repatriation of management and professional employees. Consistent with the needs for international staffing, organization units should identify competent employees who have the desire and potential to successfully undertake an assignment abroad.

Guidelines: 1. Pre-assignment Pre-assignment orientation program should be planned and implemented on a timely basis to assure that candidates and their dependents are fully prepared to undertake international assignments. Organization units assigning personnel internationally will define in writing all known conditions of assignment, including but not limited to the employee's salary, allowances, duration of assignment, etc. The employee should be provided copies of all applicable policies and procedures. 2. Repatriation and reassignment-Organization units should periodically review the status of their international assignees and develop specific repatriation plans for each employee. Where performance continues to be satisfactory, it is the responsibility of these units to assure that personnel selected for international assignments will have upon return a position at least equivalent to the level held by the employee prior to accepting the international assignment. For coordination reasons, it is also the responsibility of these units to keep Key Personnel Services advised of their repatriation plans or problems. 3. Application-This procedure applies to all organization units assigning personnel internationally, as well as to all management and professional personnel who accept an international assignment, with the exception of those engaged in service and other activities which normally require international travel or who are assigned for a limited time to specific international customer contracts abroad.

Abroad as at home, poor supervision and inappropriate policies produce negative results.

Deficiencies in management away from home can be costly. More and more attention, therefore, is likely to be given to recruiting, selecting, developing, and motivating managers for overseas assignments, however brief the assignment.

Tung suggest that to enhance expatriate success and minimize failure, U.S. multinationals (1) adopt a longer-term orientation with regard to expatriate assignments and provide support mechanisms at corporate headquarters to allay concerns about repatriation, (2) develop a more international orientation, and (3) provide more rigorous training programs to prepare expatriates for cross-cultural encounters.

Implementing policy guidelines

The first step after formulating a policy for the management of both expatriates and third country nationals is the pursuit of this policy to administer adequately the selection, orientation and training, compensation, and placement procedures inaugurated for salespeople for position away from home."

Selection

Selection is crucial to the success for an overseas appointment. It is desirable to establish adequate selection criteria and to adapt the criteria carefully to ensure that the right person is chosen. Potential candidates could be rated as either satisfactory or unsatisfactory on each of the criteria listed. Then the person showing the highest satisfactory ratings overall could be the final choice. In addition to the factors included in the sample list, the candidate's spouse should be involved in the selection process right from the start. Many failures stem form the spouse's reluctance to transfer in the first place and an inability to adapt to host country conditions. An expatriate rated as having a marginal chance of success might do very well because of supportive selection system. Further before accepting the assignment, the candidate and his or her spouse should be given an opportunity to see the county. An advance trip of a week or so cannot give anyone a through understanding of a country's culture, but, if properly done, it enables the prospective expatriate to make a more intelligent decision.

Interview criteria for international candidates

motivation

- Investigate reasons and degree of interest in wanting to be considered.
- Determine desire to work abroad, verified by previous concerns such as personal travel, language training, reading, and association with foreign employees or students.
- Determine whether the candidate has a realistic understanding of what working and living abroad requires.
- Determine the basic attitudes of the spouse toward an overseas assignment

Health

- Determine whether any medical problems of

the candidate or family might interfere with the success of the assignment.

- Determine whether the candidate is in good physical and mental health, without any foreseeable change.

Language ability

- Determine potential for learning a new language.
- Determine any previous language(s) studied or oral ability .
- Determine the ability of the spouse to meet the language requirements.

Family considerations

- How may moves has the family made in the past between different cities or parts of the Unites States?
- What problems were encountered?
- How recent was the last move?
- What is the spouse's goal in this move?
- What is the number of children and the age of each?
- Has divorce or its potential, death of a family member, etc., weakened family solidarity?
- Will all the children move why, why not?
- What are the location health and living arrangements of grandparents and the number of trips normally made to their home(s) each year?

- Are there any special adjustment problems that you would expect?
- How is each member of the family reaching to this possible move?
- Do special educational problems exist within the family?

Resourcefulness and initiative

- Is the candidate independent: can the candidate make and stand by decision and judgments?
- Does the candidate have the intellectual capacity to deal with several dimensions simultaneously?
- Is the candidate able to reach objectives and produce results with available personnel and facilities, regardless of the limitations and barriers that might arise?
- Can the candidate operate without a clear definition of responsibility and authority on a foreign assignment?
- Will the candidate be able to explain the aims and company philosophy to the ideal managers and workers?

Resourcefulness and initiative

- Does the candidate possess sufficient self-reliance, self-0discipline, and self-confidence to overcome difficulties or handle complex problems?

- Can the candidate work without supervision?
- Can the candidate operate effectively in a foreign environment without normal communication and supporting services?

Adaptability

- Is the candidate sensitive to others, open to the opinions of others, cooperative and able to compromise?
- What are the candidate's reactions to new situations, and efforts to understand and appreciate differences?
- Is the candidate culturally sensitive, aware, and able to relate across the culture?
- Does the candidate understand his own culturally derived values?
- How does the candidate react to criticism?
- What is the candidate's understanding of the U.S. government system?
- Will the candidate be able to make and develop contacts with his peers in the foreign country?
- Does the candidate have patience when dealing with problems?
- Is the candidate resilient can be bounce back after setbacks?

Career planning

- Does the candidate consider the assignment anything other than a temporary overseas trip?

- Is the move consistent with the candidate's progression and that planned by the company?
- Is the candidate's career planning realistic?
- What is the candidate's basic attitude toward the company?
- Is there any history or indication of personnel problems with this employee?

Financial

- Are there any current financial and/or legal considerations which might affect the assignment, e.g., house purchase, children and college expenses, car purchases?
- Are financial considerations negative factors, i.e., will undue pressures be brought to bear on the employee or family as a result of the assignment?

Orientation and training

Sales personnel slated for foreign assignment should be oriented to the new job and provided relevant training. Essentially, orientation and training should cover the terms and conditions of the assignment, language training, and cultural training.

Terms and conditions of the assignment: The employee should be provided with a clear and concise overview of the company's expatriate policies and procedures, compensation system; information on housing, transportation, and schools in the host country; and information on moving arrangements.

Language training: Language training is perhaps the most basic type of knowledge that a foreigner needs for a productive life in a host country. Language is the key to a country's culture. It permits understanding of the subtleties of the country and the reasons why certain things are done differently. A language can be learned in different ways: in a language school with a regular program lasting several months; through a short, intensive program offered either by a commercial school or a local university or at home through a self-study program. Do-it-yourself kits are available for home study programs in the form of records, cassette recordings, books, telephone conversations with instructors, and different combinations of these alternatives. Regardless of the method, the one central ingredient in learning a language is proper motivation in the part of the employee and family. It is incumbent upon the multinational employer to emphasize the need for language training.

Cultural training: Both academic and interpersonal cultural training should be given. Academic training includes the provision of things like books, maps, brochures, films, and slides. The interpersonal training consists of making arrangements for candidate and family to make a trip to the host county, in addition to meeting with host country natives living in the United States and people who have lived previously in the host country.

Compensation

Salespeople away form their home phase cost

more because they must be paid extra compensation. The extra compensation covers three factors. First, it is a premium for climatic conditions in the host country, separation from friends and relatives, cultural shock, and subjection to situations of political instability and economic risk in conditions of unstable currencies. Second, it is an allowance for housing, children's schooling, return trips home on a periodic basis, income tax, and overall cost-of-living expenses. Third, there are certain perquisites common in host countries for particular positions, like car and driver, servants, and club memberships.

The element of compensation and the amount paid under each heading differ from country to country. The table shows what it takes to maintain a $110,000-a-year U.S. lifestyle for a family of four in different cities around the world. For example, in Hong Kong another $49,051 will be needed to support the same living, while in Mexico one will end up saving over $6,000.

The figure illustrates a typical expatriate compensation package. Note that the total additional compensation is over three times more in Indonesia than in Brazil, although both are developing countries. The difference is accounted for by demand and supply conditions relative to different elements of compensation. In a city like Tokyo, housing would be very expensive since suitable apartments are very scarce. In many developing countries, housing is expensive because Western style accommodations are difficult to locate, and a high premium must be paid for the fee that are available. Similarly, if taxes are very high in country

Living Expense Differences in Various Cities in the World

City	Housing	Transpo-rtation	Taxes	Goods and services	Total
Hone Kong	$52,360	$15,878	$8,100	$12,713	$89,051
Tokyo	39,487	6,233	15,650	18,435	79,805
Geneva	22,667	5,674	19,983	17,397	65,721
Brussels	9,193	5,228	36,883	13,502	64,806
Frankfurt	12,345	5,518	25,989	14,628	58,480
Buenos Aires	19,103	4,854	21,016	10,596	55,569
Sydney	12,192	9,620	18,860	13,268	52,940
Paris	15,199	4,786	18,886	13,098	51,969
Amsterdam	11,014	5,081	19,723	13,508	49,326
London	15,269	6,254	10,681	13,846	46,050
Rio de Janerio	13,703	4,216	14,748	1,125	43,792
Mexico City	8,175	2,893	12,480	10,139	33,687

Considering the expenses involved in transferring nonnative to host countries, the company should make a careful study of the conditions of each country and undertake regular reviews of any changes. The overhead to keep watch on the changes in costs, taxation, facilities, and currency values is by no means negligible; experts in the field are high-priced, and their travel budgets are large. Nevertheless the cost is a sound investment if as a result the company's team of valuable expatriates and/or third country nationals is fairly compensated and has confidence in the home office's policy toward them. These necessary perquisites secure their profitable contribution to the company's performance.

Placement

Once a salesperson accepts an overseas position, the company should provide adequate information to prepare for the departure to the host country. This information includes advice on such matters as how to apply for passport; how to obtain necessary visas and immunizations; how expenses should be handled for reimbursement; how to obtain transportation and arrange accompanied baggage and unaccompanied baggage shipment; tax matters; and current status under the various company benefit plans, pension, stock, and insurance. Information is also needed on obtaining an international driver's license, making financial arrangements, deciding what clothing to take, and even reminding the salesperson to notify correspondents of a change of address. Some of these arrangements and notify correspondents of a change of address. Some of these arrangements and details are quite complicated, and generous advice and council for each individual can smooth the passage of personnel and their families to transfer assignments.

Repatriation and reassignment

Traditionally, salespeople have welcomed overseas assignments. It has meant taking extra compensation and seeing the world at company expense; besides, going abroad was considered to be a route to the executive suite. More recently, however, fewer jobs are opening up in Euro-Capitals. The Middle East and the LDCs are the new foreign-assignment destinations, where hardship pay lives up to its name and the experience offers little beyond just that-experience. A returning salesperson faces a severe penalty for being out of the home office working environment and a severe shock when confronted with the domestic real estate market.

Fewer salespeople are willing to accept overseas positions, particularly those personnel who perceive the risk of an inferior position upon return. On a number of occasions, there has been no job for a returning expatriate, who has then spent months in a holding pattern. Many companies lose good salespeople for lack of job vacancies in the United States when their time comes to return.

Returning home amounts to facing previously familiar surroundings. Yet, as the following quotes show, expatriates have found the reentry into the home environment more of a problem than going abroad.

Repatriating executives from overseas assignments is a top management challenge that goes far beyond the superficial problems and costs of physical relocation. The crux of the matter is the assumption that since these individuals are returning home-that is, to a familiar way of life-they have no trouble adapting to either the corporate or the home environment. However, experience has shown that repatriation is anything but simple.

Managers know that there is always a risk of being stuck at least temporarily, in a mediocre job when they return.

Few, if any executives ever come out ahead financially in a transfer back to the U.S. An even more serious shock, because it can have a long-range impact on the executive's career, is the re-adaptation to corporate life a foreign assignment keep the executive out of the mainstream of advancement. In some respects the more outstanding a performer the executive was overseas, the more uncomfortable his return will be.

The returning executives themselves have made these comments:

> Going home is a harder move. The foreign move has the excitement of being new more confusing, but exciting. Reentry is frightening I'll be happy to be home I wonder if I can adjust back.

The repatriation problem is not limited to U.S. expatriates. Even Japanese returnees find it hard to assimilate their own culture after having spent a few years in the United States. Because most Japanese white-collar workers generally have a negative attitude toward overseas assignments, many returnees end up taking jobs with the U.S. subsidiaries in Japan.

To alleviate the reluctance of personnel to be recruited for foreign assignments, companies are providing prospective expatriates with written guarantees on company foreign personnel policy. These repatriation agreements are really no more than general promises in writing that include a limit of a two-to five-year maximum on time spent abroad and assurances of return to a mutually acceptable job. Union Carbibe assigns senior executives to act as sponsors for overseas managers, including salespeople. Sponsors scout six months prior to the expatriates' return to locate a suitable position. Union Carbide's Linde division has a seven member committee to review overseas personnel and place returning employees. The Dow Chemical Company has ten full-time counselors who visit with each of the company's expatriate employees, including those in sales, once a year. The counselors let the expatriates know that they have not been forgotten and act as advocates for possible promotion considerations. Also, repatriation supervisors are assigned to expatriates to monitor compensation, performance, and potential career paths.

At Westinghouse, the originating suborganization assumes responsibility for placement of returning individuals in positions of appropriate responsibility at the conclusion of foreign assignments. Each expatriate receives a formal performance evaluation. If deemed unsatisfactory, the employee will simply be repatriated with no new position. If the review is acceptable, the employee will receive reasonable assurances of a position upon returning and will be counseled on the potential for promotion. The repatriation process begins with the identification of a new home position six months prior to the completion of the out-of-country assignment. Westinghouse also places its overseas personnel on a computerized corporate file that matches expatriates' qualifications with job openings.

The results of repatriation programs exhibit a pattern of success. The success rate in getting overseas personnel to remain in their posts for the duration of the assignment is much when a satisfactory repatriation policy exists. It alleviates possible career anxieties.

Salespeople with international experience are an invaluable corporate asset. Repatriation agreements should ensure that the experience gained by personnel through such assignments is retained and properly utilized.

Adler's empirical work on he subject shown that a few ad hoc measures are not enough to remove the problems of the returnees.

Predeparture training: Since employees who adjust well overseas tend to be more effective at reentry, organizational should provide predeparture training for employees and their families.

Selection: Employees who are successful and satisfied prior to going overseas tend to be successful and satisfied at reentry. Sending failures will not bring home successes. It is therefore recommended that organizations select effective, rather than marginal employees for overseas assignments.

Overseas contact: Foreign-based employees who are aware of both the positive and negative changes in the organization tend to be more effective are reentry. It is recommended that management frequently inform foreign based employees of current organization policies, projects, plans, etc.

Job responsibility: The higher the job responsibility at reentry, the more effective is the returnee. It is recommended that reentry be planned rom the employee's career perspective and not solely according toe the demand of the overseas project

Cross-cultural skills: Because awareness of cross-cultural skills is often tacit and because skills are often seen as not transferable to the home country, it is recommended that returnees be assisted in identifying their newly enhanced and acquired skills, and in finding ways to apply them within the home organization.

Xenophobic home country managers: Since mangers who have to worked in foreign countries frequently discount the value of the returnees' overseas experience, it is recommended that the home organization assist home country managers in recognizing and developing ways to use returnees cross-cultural skills.

Similar countries: Since reentry from all parts of the world can be equally difficult, it is recommended that reentry form more similar countries be as well managed as reentry from more dissimilar countries.

External validation: Since returnees whose experience is recognized and valued by the organization are more effective and use their cross-culturally acquired skills to a greater extent, and since a xenophobic response is common among home country managers, it is recommended that home country managers be taught how to value returnees and their foreign experiences.

Actually, a systematic approach, which takes care of expatriates right from the beginning, is needed to resolve the repatriation problem. Harvey suggest a four phased program for this purpose.

1. Planning expatriation

Development of foreign assignment with specific objectives in mind.

2, Preexpatriation phase

Clear delineation/communication of executive's objectives in foreign assignments

Development of consensus on evaluation criteria for foreign assignments . Information/awareness of repatriation problems

Provision of necessary training for family and executive for foreign assignment.

3. Expatriation phase

Establishment/maintenance of formal communication channels with expatriate

Supply of data on domestic activities and the importance of expatriate's assignments

Systematic/periodic review of expatriate's foreign assignment

Performance/evaluation o expatriate an adequate recognition/money

Assessment of domestic job opportunities and their fit into career path of expatriate

4. Repatriation phase

Intensive organization/environment update for executive

Redefinition of motivation for domestic position

Assistance with family reorientation

Movement of sales people across national boundaries for temporary assignment in another country is most likely to continue. These people are of significant vale. They serve as catalysts of new ideas and as risk takers the MINC's people on the spot, so to speak. companies must undertake proper measures to equip them for ultimate gains and success in the foreign environments and bring them home for the ultimate gain of the corporation and their continued happiness and success in it.

Foreign sales promotion

Sales promotion devices tend to stimulate new attitudes toward the promoted product through the lure of getting something for nothing. The very feeling that something can be had for free creates a strong desire for the product among buyers no matter which country/region they belong to. Historically, sales promotion is a uniquely American phenomenon. But today sales promotion techniques are popularly used to supplement advertising and personal selling throughout the Free World.

Besides increasing sales at the retail level, sales promotion helps in building the morale of the sales force. Some companies use sales promotion simultaneously with sales incentive schemes to make them complement each other. For example in the 1970s. Hoover company promoted its vacuum cleaners in England through providing a packet of one dozen throw-away vacuum bags as a lure. At the same time the company organized a sales contest for its dealers and sales force for a vacation inthe United States. Sales promotion also acts as a push-through device by making customers want the product. Once the image of a product is established among customers, dealers, and retailers will be compelled to stock it. For example, Coca-Cola Company introduced its orange soda, Fanta, in many developing countries through free gifts of ballpoint pens and pencils and the like. Through consumer demand even the very small retailers were forced into carrying Fanta.

Devices of sales promotion can be classified on the basis of the function to be performed and the target to be reached. Three main types of sales promotion functions can be distinguished: sales promotion for introducing a new product, sales promotion for increasing the use of a product, and sales promotion for the direct enticement of customers at retail level. Free samples price-off coupons, direct enticement of customers at retail leave. Free samples price-off coupons, and refund offers are the devices used for introducing new products price-off deals, premiums, contests, and sweepstakes constitute the methods for securing greater use of a product. Trading stamps, retailer coupons, and point-of purchase demonstrations are resorted to for action at the retail level. Sales promotion demonstrations are resorted to for action at the retail level. Sales promotion techniques can be consumer oriented, and dealer- and distributor-oriented. Sampling, demonstrations, or instructions, premium offers or temporary price reductions; and contests and sweepstakes are consumer-oriented promotion devices. Intermediary-or agent-oriented techniques will include assistance in store layout, assistance in planning an developing strategy such as accounting and inventory instructions, cooperative advertising dealers' sales training, provision of point-of-purchase materials, and money and merchandise allowances.

The above categorization is based on U.S. practices. Marketing environment in a foreign market however, may require making appropriate adaptation is sales promotion offerings. As a matter of fact, in some nations a marketer may be forced into coming out with an entirely new sales promotion idea that is in line with the country's environment. Poor economic conditions in developing countries may suggest putting greater emphasis on the economic value of the offering, assuming the product is directed at the mass market. Legal restrictions in many countries call for adptation. In West Germany, giveaways are legally prohibited. Further, the sales promotion campaign should not create conflict in the marketplace so as to raise eyebrows in political circles. Inasmuch as some sales promotion campaign. For example, retailers in most developing countries are small, scattered, and disorganized. They may not be able to handle the equivalent of cents-off type of sales promotion. Above all, the sales promotion offering should be culturally acceptable. The customization of sales promotion to match the perspectives of a country is well illustrated by Ford Motor Company's efforts in BRazil. In the midst of high inflation, banks in Brazil were not willing to finance purchase of big-price items by low-income families. For Motor Company, therefore, established car-buying clubs of sixty members each. Each member made sixty monthly payments toward a car. A drawing was held each month and the member whose name appeared on the drawing received the car that month. This way the low-income Brazilian families continued to buy the cars without being burdened with high interest costs. The company, on the other hand, generated a guaranteed number of customers such month.

Management of sales promotion requires (1) a clear definition of objectives; (2) making budget allocations (3) drawing a plan of action covering such points as length of the campaign, details of sales promotions offering, instructions required for the sales force and middle agents, coordination needed with other departments of the company, media announcements, and cost estimates; and (4) an evaluation of the campaign to determine its viability for future use in the same country, and in other nations.

Public relations overseas

Public relations serves as a useful device for establishing a foothold and/or strengthening existing position in an overseas market. The public relations activity is directed toward an influential, though relatively small, target audience of editors and journalists who work for publications or in broadcasting aimed at a firm's customers and prospects. Since the target audience is small, it is relatively in expensive to reach.

To do an effective public relations job overseas, an international marketer needs to hire an established public relations firm. It is desirable to look for a firm that has relevant experience and adequate resources. If the United STates public relations firm is recruited, the company should develop a dossier, that is, a package of information that editors may file for future reference. A typical dossier runs to ten pages and incudes information on the company's capabilities, its technologies, its preeminence, na why it operates in the host country. The dossier may be supplemented with a corporate brochure, preferably in the host country language, identifying worldwide manufacturing, research and development, and sales/service locations. Usually, the dossier is accompanied by a letter inviting editors to contact a designated person for further information. The letter may also state that articles and releases will be regularly issued by the company in the future.

The company should decide, in consultation with the public relations firm, how an initial contact should be made with the target audience, editors, and journalists. At this stage, the public relations firm is better know to the audience than is its client. As a matter of fact, some public relations firm are so well accepted in a country that a release on the company's behalf signals editors that the story is newsworthy, factual, and worth publishing. Thus, the public relations firm should play a lead role in establishing initial contact for the firm.

Future announcements and releases may either be custom-developed for the host country or extracted from among those prepared for the domestic market.

4 Promotion and Distribution Strategy

Promotion is essentially an exercise in *communications*. Mac-Donald's may have the most tasty, low-priced hamburger in town, but unless they can communicate this information to the public, their success will be limited. MacDonald's has, of course, recognized the importance of effective communication, and this has been one of the major keys to their success.

All communication involves a source, channel, and receiver. The *source* may be a person, a group, or an institution, such as a business. In marketing, the source may take on a number of forms, such as an advertising message or a salesman. The *channel* is the medium or carrier of the communication. In the case of an advertising message, the channel could be a billboard, a TV commercial, or a magazine ad. The *receiver* is the object for whom the source has intended the message. An individual consumer, groups of people, or an institution may be recipients of marketing communications.

As an exercise in communication, promotion is any means of informing, persuading, and reminding consumers about all aspects of the firm and its products and services. The promotion may be designed to generate an immediate or deferred response from consumers. When Sears holds their "After Christmas Sale," their goal is to have people flock to the store immediately. On the other hand, energy conservation advertising by the petroleum companies is designed, in part, to build long-term good will on the public's part toward the company.

The marketer has at his disposal a number of promotional tools. The job becomes one of selecting the most strategic combination of these tools. To be more specific, various combinations of *advertising, personal selling, sales promotion, packaging, branding, public relations,* and *publicity* may be chosen. Although each of these promotional elements communicates to the buyer, the following pages will show that each has different characteristics.

Generally, the two most significant elements in promotion strategy are advertising and personal selling. In terms of communication, advertising enables a single source to reach numerous receivers. The receivers of the message may, however, either "tune-in" or "tune-out" the advertisement. Personal selling, on the other hand, consists of a one-to-one relationship between the source and the receiver. Even though fewer consumers are reached, the effectiveness of the communication typically exceeds the results of advertising to a large anonymous audience because personal selling provides for a two-way communication flow between the seller and buyer. The impersonal nature of advertising prohibits this type of direct interaction.

Advertising

Advertising may be defined as "the impersonal communication of ideas, goods, or services, to a mass audience by an identified paying sponsor." Broad advertising objectives might include an increase in sales volume, or an increase in market share. Looked at differently, the objectives of advertising are to increase awareness of, increase interest in, generate a trial of, or hasten adoption of the product or service. Rather specific advertising objectives might also exist. For example, a campaign might be aimed at increasing attendance at an upcoming rock concert, improving the flow of goods in the channel of distribution, or simply generating inquiries about a product.

Given a set of advertising objectives, strategies for achieving them must then be formulated. These strategic decisions are made in two basic areas: copy strategy and media strategy.

Copy strategy is the actual message, but includes more than just what is said; that is, how the message is conveyed, its style, its design. The effectiveness of the advertising message is highly dependent on copy strategy. The writing and artistic skills involved suggest that technical expertise and creativity are required to develop quality copy.

Media strategy involves the choice of channels through which advertising messages flow. Despite the prominence of television advertising, the major medium for advertising expenditures in newspapers. Approximately one-third of all expenditures to newspapers, followed in order by television, direct mail, radio, and magazines.

Strategic decisions: Determining the appropriate copy and media are important advertising decisions. The following factors should be considered in making these decisions: *market characteristics, product attributes,* and *cost.*

Market characteristics should be uppermost in the advertiser's mind when marketing copy and media decisions. the objective should be to match the copy and media to the targeted consumer group.

Distribution of Advertising expenditures by media

Media	Percent of Total	Dollar Expenditures
		(Millions of $)
Newspapers	30.2	$6,960
Television	17.9	4,110
Direct Mail	14.5	3,350
Radio	6.6	1,530
Magazines	6.4	1,480
Business Papers	3.3	770
Outdoor	1.3	290
Miscellaneous	19.7	4,541
	99.9	$23,031

Product attributes may also dictate particular decisions. Copy illustrating how the camera functions has been necessary for most Polaroid advertisements. The company has also found that television and selected magazines are the best media for communicating their messages. Women's cosmetics make use of a similar media combination because of the necessity of conveying a multicolored, visual message.

Cost is obviously an important determinant in copy and media selection. no firm has unlimited advertising dollars, and this element of promotion can be expensive. A full page ad in *Cosmopolitan* magazine, for example, costs over $8,000 for one issue; the same size ad in the *Wall Street Journal* costs over $22,000. Interestingly enough, the two publications have similar circulations. In assessing cost, a firm should look at both absolute and relative figures. Actual dollar outlays would show, for instance, that television is considerably more expensive than having the same copy communicated in several newspapers. But is this all that should be considered? Obviously, the relative cost-the comparison between the absolute cost and the number of customers reached by the message-is also important. The significance of relative costs indicates why marketers are often willing to spend more on a particular media.

Use of agencies: Because of the specialized nature of advertising, many firms use the services of advertising agencies. These experts often assist companies in the creative and technical aspects of advertising, including idea creation, copy and art work, media evaluation, and production. To a lesser extent, a firm's agency may also offer services in marketing research, sales promotion, merchandising, and public relations. Although many activities may be "farmed out" to an agency, all firms should have someone within th organization to oversee and give direction to this important element of promotion strategy.

Personal selling

The virtue of advertising is that it is very economical forms of communication in terms of the number of people reached per dollar spent. Personal selling, on the other hand, is quite costly per individual or firm contacted. The advantage of personal selling is that it can approach the market on a much more selective basis and benefit from the one-to-one interaction.

Personal selling may be defined as "oral presentation in a conversation with one or more prospective purchasers for the purpose of making a sale." It has often been said about business that nothing happens until someone sells something to someone else. That statement is as true today as it ever was. The United States Census Bureau statistics show that almost 10 percent of the total U.S. labor force is involved in sales. When it is understood that the Bureau is likely to put many persons who are primarily personal sellers into other classifications, it is quite possible that more than 10 percent of the nation's labor force, or over 7 million people, are engaged in personal selling.

The role of the salesperson may be described

in many ways. One of the most appropriate involves a classification of selling situations. The classification of selling situations. The classification includes:

1. Situations in which the salesperson's job is primarily to deliver a product e.g., driver salesperson for soft drinks, milk, bread, fuel oil.
2. Situations in which the salesperson is primarily an inside order taker: e.g., the the retail clerk.
3. Situations in which the salesperson is primarily an outside order taker going to the customer in the field; e.g., a packing house, soap, or spice salesperson.
4. Situations in which the salesperson is not expected or permitted to solicit an order-the job is to build goodwill, perform promotional activities, or provide services for the customer. This type of salesperson is often called the missionary salesperson, and may represent a distiller, an ethical pharmaceutical manufacturer, or similar occupations.
5. Situations in which the major emphasis is placed upon the salesperson's technical knowledge; e.g., a salesperson with an engineering background who is primarily consultant to the customer.
7. Situations in which intangibles such as insurance, advertising, services, of communications systems are sold.

These situations have been arranged in a hierarchy of increasing complexity. A perusal of the list indicates that the talents required of the sellers vary dramatically with the nature of the selling job.A situation not included in the above classification has recently emerged. Since 1974 economic conditions have created significant shortages in major portions of the economy. the obvious question is, what does a salesperson do when there is nothing to sell? The answer would appear to be "drum up supplies" for favored customers whether they are products of the seller's own company or not.

A drilling big company increase needed a huge quantity of steel plate and went to Ducomman. In the big Los Angles based metals distribution. Ducomman could not fill the order from normal sources but rather than leave a customer in the torch a Ducommun salesperson went to work as a temporaries purchasing a gent and finally lined up a Rumanian source. "If out customer had not gotten that steel plate." Said Charles K. Preston. Ducommun Executive Vice President." he would have been unable to make production schedules. We figure customers will remember this kind of extra service once it's not quite such a sellers' market."

Unfortunately, the public's view of sellers is often colored by the behavior of the state-fair huckster and the used car salesman. Most of today's sellers, particularly those marketing nonhousehold goods, are professionals. They are attuned to their customers' needs and familiar with the intricate attributes of their products and services. Salespersons working for companies such as IBM and Proctor and Gamble serve their customers almost as quasi-consultants. they recognize that their own success as sales professionals is intimately tied to the satisfaction their customers derive from their products and services.

In combination with advertising, personal selling forms the core of promotion strategy. It is primarily through these two techniques that the prospect is initially made aware of a product and service and later sold. After examining the other elements of promotional strategy, the coordination of advertising and personal selling will be discussed.

Other forms of promotion

There are several other promotion elements in addition to advertising and personal selling. As indicated previously, these are sales promotion, branding and packaging, public relations, and publicity.

Sales promotion: These activities are designed to complement advertising and personal selling. Sales promotion can be defined as "those marketing activities other than personal selling, advertising, and publicity that stimulate consumer purchasing and dealer effectiveness, such as displays, shows and exhibitions, demonstrations, and various non-recurring selling efforts not in the ordinary routine."

While sales promotion is ordinarily viewed as a complementary type of promotional activity, its importance should not be underestimated. Sales promotion expenditures in industrialized economies have been variously estimated at between 20 and 35 percent of total promotional budgets. Consider, for example, the impact of coupons.

The shopping public is being deluged with coupons as never before. A.C. Nielson, the biggest of the coupon cleaning houses, notes that in 1966 manufacturers issued 12.8 billion coupons. That figure more than doubled by 1973 to 27.6 billion and Nielson predicts another 15 percent rise atop this in 1974-to 31.5 billion. The big surge of late has come in retailers own in-ad coupons. No one knows how many will be printed this year, but estimates range from a conservative 20 billion to 40 billion and up.

Far-fetched? Consider the possibilities. One chain running, six in-ad coupons a week in the Philadelphia Inquirer would publish 66,174,000 coupons a year. Direct mail flyers and shopper newspapers would add millions more Results between manufacturers and retailers 50 billion of the little money saving certificates will be printed by year's end-more than 15 for every man, woman and child on the globe."

Branding and packaging: These elements are a part of the promotional mix in that both brand and package communicate information and images about the product to the public. A brand is a "word, mark, symbol, design, term, or a combination of these, both visual and oral, used for the purpose of identification of some product or service. "The communication functions of packaging are several. For instance, the package attracts attention, provides distinctiveness, influences attitudes by its design and physical attributes, facilitates display through its shape, and informs. Brands perform certain functions for the promotional strategist. Specifically, the brand permits product identification, differentiation, and distinctiveness.

Promote a new product without National advertising and pass savings on to the consumer? that's what new York-based Witco Chemical Corp. is trying with its new detergent, Active. The box, not TV commercials, sells, Witco says. Box copy reads: "Active cleans as well as leading nationally advertised all-purpose laundry detergents. Active can be sold for less than most nationally advertised detergents because Active is not nationally advertised." To induce consumers, to look for the box, Witco and its agency, Ries Cappiello Colwell. New York hired spokes women to appear on TV and radio talk shows and before consumerist groups and will furnish material for columns in newspapers and women's magazines. May be today's consumer is so fed up with the volume of repetitive advertising in a product category like laundry detergents cat a time when Tide is spending 810 million and Cheer $8 million that she or he is ready to buy a non-advertised brand."

Public relations: An important part of a successful promotion is public relations strategy. this term may be defined as: "the activities of a corporation, union, government, or other organization in building and maintaining sound productive relations with special publics, such as customers, employees, or stockholders, and with the public at large so as to adapt itself to its environment, and interpret itself to society." The field of public relations is today maturing and assuming new dimensions. Following the marketing philosophy of management, the public relations function must be tuned to the marketplace, must be responsive to ends, and must communicate its response to an interested public(s).

Publicity: This final, but by no means least important, element of promotion strategy is the "non-personal stimulation of demand for a product, service, or business unit by planting commercially significant news about it in a published medium or obtaining favorable presentation of it on radio, television, or stage, that is not paid for by the sponsor." Publicity can be managed and it is a valuable supplement to advertising and personal selling. Since a newsworthy item is not identified with a sponsor, it has the aura of objectivity that is often missing in advertising. Furthermore, there is generally no direct cost to the firm in that the communication is accepted by the medium as a news item as opposed to an advertisement.

Coordinating the promotional elements

While each of the previously discussed promotional techniques is separate and distinct, and effective promotional strategy orchestrates the elements into a coordinated communications effort. Potential disaster may exist, for example, when the sales force is unfamiliar with the firm's advertising messages.

A major bank in the South constructed a beautiful new headquarters building in the mid-1970s. While under construction, the structure was surrounded by an ugly construction fence. Since the evolving structure and fence were somewhat of an eyesore, the advertising people at the bank decided to do something about it. A campaign was introduced, primarily through newspaper ads, to encourage interested individuals to paint a portion of the fence. The only requirements to participate were that (a) what was painted had to have a bicentennial theme, and (b) a person had to fill out a short form "available at any branch" prior to beginning work on the fence. It was here that the coordination between advertising and personal selling broke down.

All promotion elements utilized should be communicating a consistent message to the marketplace.

In considering promotion as a whole, the firm must determine the relative usage of each of the available elements. This is not easy, but some obvious rules of thumb are apparent. In marketing

Crest, Proctor and Gamble places primary emphasis on advertising. Honeywell's computer division, on the other hand, allocates most of its promotional dollars to personal selling. Factors such as the nature of the market, funds available, nature of the product, and its stage in the life cycle should be considered in determining the relative usage of the various elements. Advertising is generally considered the primary promotional tool in marketing consumer goods, whereas personal selling occupies the most important position in nonhousehold goods. This practice should not imply, however, that advertising is unimportant in nonhousehold marketing and personal selling is unimportant in household marketing. The Honeywell computer salesman would be in a vulnerable position if a prospective client responded, "Honeywell sells computers? I didn't know that." The salesman depends on advertising to create an awareness among prospects that Honeywell does indeed market computers.

The macro environment and promotion strategy

Many forces *outside* the firm influence the formulation of promotion strategy. the macro environment establishes constraints as well as opportunities for a company. The ability of the firm to adapt its communications to the changing institutional, international, sociocultural, economic, legal, competitive, and technological environments will help determine the results of its marketing effort. For this reason, the astute organization will continually monitor the macro environment, noting the changes that suggest adjustments in promotional strategy.

Marketers of feminine hygiene products have substantially altered their marketing communications after careful investigation of the sociocultural environment. Changing life styles and a new "openness" in society have broadened the acceptable promotional alternatives for these companies. Once limited to a select number of women's magazines, feminine hygiene products are now advertised on television and in campus newspapers.

Economic, competitive, and international forces necessitated major adjustments by American automotive companies in recent years. Public concern over fuel economy and competitive inroads by foreign producers led the Chevrolet Division of General Motors to introduce the Chevette a year ahead of schedule. While Ford, Chrysler, and AMC would have liked to have had a new 1976 subcompact available, it should be noted that chevrolet's "one-upsmanship" occurred in part because the Chevette had been marketed in South America prior to its domestic introduction. the introductory promotion of the Chevette stressed its excellent fuel economy and positioned the product head-to-head with the major economy imports.

Distribution strategy

Once the product has been created, priced, and promoted, means must be found to place the product in the hands of the ultimate consumer. Distribution strategy involves getting the product to the customer *when* he wants it and *where* he wants it.

Distribution strategy can be divided into two areas of investigation. The first area involves the development of a channel through which the product will flow, and the second area involves the physical movement of products through the channel.

Channel strategy: A channel of distribution may be defined as "the structure of intra company organization units and extra-company agents and dealers, wholesale and retail, through which a commodity, product or service is marketed." The typical channel is made up of the manufacturing organization and one or more intermediaries. The second consumer products channel has experienced the greatest growth in the past decade. In the industrial products channel, the manufacturer to industrial user alternative is the most significant.

In an advanced economy such as the United states, middlemen exist to *concentrate, sort* and *disperse* products between manufacturers and ultimates consumers.

Assume for a movement that no middleman exist. a housewife is preparing a shopping list that includes Crest toothpaste, Coca-cola, Fritos corn chips, and a six pack of Schlitz. how is she going to purchase these products without middlemen? If she is in hurry, it may be best for her to get airline reservations that would route her to Cincinnati and then on to Atlanta, Dallas and Milwaukee.

The middleman, be it a wholesaler, retailer, or agent, *concentrates* products from geographically dispersed manufacturers' *sorts* the merchandise into salable units; and subsequently *disperses* the products to the ultimate consumer. One or more middlemen may be eliminated from the channel, but these three functions still have to be performed. In Sears' channels of distribution, the wholesaler has essentially been eliminated, but Sears has assumed the functions of concentrating, sorting, and dispersing. Regardless of the intermediaries involved, the following concepts hold true for distribution channels:

1. Exchange involves negotiation of terms of trade between parties.
2. Middlemen interposed between the producer and the ultimate consumer can improve the efficiency of the economic system.
3. In an industrial economy, producers and ultimate consumers seldom confront each other directly. Most products are handled by one or more middlemen.
4. In addition to products themselves, channels accommodate follows of use rights payment and information.
5. he flow between a producer and a buyer must occur if exchange transactions are to be consummated. Channel length and complexity, therefore, depend upon the effectiveness and the efficiency of the middlemen who manage the various flows.

Channel organization: A basic decision faced by the marketing manager is how to organize vertical relationships in the channel in such a way that the return to the organization will be greatest. Note that this is a decision that takes place at every channel level. Note, too, that in some cases the channel member may have no opportunity to make this decision, but rather must respond to the dictates of a more powerful member.

The ability to create, control, or influence other members in the channel is a function of many factors. These factors are largely economic and have to do with the impact of the effect of participating in the channel versus some other alternative.

Until the energy shortage, the major petroleum companies sold excess gasoline to the small independents at a price that would allow the independents to offer the gasoline for sale several cents per gallon below the price charged by their larger competitors. As oil became scarce, however, this source of supply dried up, and many independents were forced into bankruptcy.

In the above example, power in the channel was a direct result of the ability of the major oil producers to control supply. Similar control have such great buying power that they can virtually dictate terms to manufacturing organizations. The manufacturer can, of course, refuse to deal with the retail organization, but the potential loss of market share makes this a difficult decision to implement.

Although few relish the thought of being "controlled," certain advantages may accrue to those channel members who submit to the leadership of a more powerful channel member. Members of the channel can often reduce their risk by association with a large supplier or buyer, thus assuring a steady supply of, or demand for,l the product. Such a relationship can generate economies of scale for participants, further providing a competitive advantage.

In addition, the channel leader is often in a position to provide expertise and to share promotional expenses. A positive "halo effect" might accrue from association with a firm that has a very favorable public image. Often smaller participants in the channel are happy to have the responsibility of burdensome management decisions assumed by more knowledgeable members. There is a danger, of course, in "putting al your eggs in one basket." Should the major source of supply or demand be lost, the channel member with no alternatives is in an extremely vulnerable position.

Often the channel leader is found at the manufacturing level of the channel. This is true usually for two reasons. First, he knows his product best and has control of the manufacturing process. Second, he frequently, though not always, has greater economic power.

It can also be argued that the logical seat of power in the channel does, or at least should, reside at the retail level. Again, two reasons exist.

First, since the retailer represents the interface with the buying public, he should be in the best position to control market information and access to markets. As logical and consistent with the marketing philosophy of management as this idea might sound, however, it usually holds true only when the second source of power, economic power, is present. Sears, Penney's, Safeway, and other retailing giants can and do provide channel leadership.

The channel leader is found far less frequently at the wholesale level. This is interesting in the traditionally wholesalers dominate distribution channels. When manufacturers and retailers are both relatively small, the wholesaler often provides a critical integrative function. In the grocery industry, wholesalers such as Associated Grocers and IGA help small food retailers remain competitive with the Safeway's and A & P's.

In nonhousehold markets the manufacturer is almost always the channel leader. This is the case in part because the major channel in these markets contains no middlemen. However, even when middlemen are involved, the economic power of the manufacturers results in their assuming leadership.

Vertical channel systems. In the previous section, the basic dilemma faced by the marketing manager of whether to attempt to lead the channel or submit to the direction of others was presented. As noted, this decision is a product of a variety of economic considerations. The strategy of channel integration is really an extension of the idea of channel leadership and control. By integrating individual channel members into an organized whole, channel conflicts are ideally reduced and a common set of goals is obtained.

Vertical systems are created in three distinct ways. The most obvious way is through *direct ownership of channel members.* Companies that produce and market their products and services directly to the consumer include the Singer Corporation and Goodyear, to name but two. With ownership, of course, comes complete control.

A second form of vertical channel system is the *administered system.* This is simply a formalized extension of the channel leadership idea. Simply, when a firm can control the channel through some form of economic power, it becomes a natural next step to begin to plan integrated programs for channel members. Kraftco, for example, markets its products aggressively to consumer, and also provides display and merchandising advice to retail stores.

The third method of achieving vertical integration is through *contractual systems.* This arrangement represents the most rapid growth of the three systems and is illustrated by such organizations as MacDonald's, Ramada Inn, Midas Muffler shops, automobile corporations and their dealerships, McKesson and Robbins, and many others. Franchising is a form of contractual system. Note that in each of the three systems, leadership may come from any level of the channel.

Channel trends: Several significant changes have occurred in distribution channels i the past ten to fifteen years. In the past, once a manufacturer sold a product to a wholesaler, the latter pushed the product forward to the retailer, who in turn pushed the product to the ultimate consumer. This *push* philosophy has changed to a marked degree as a result of the channel leader being attuned to the ultimate consumers' need sand wants. Today, most channel leaders have adopted a *pull* philosophy, which suggests that the leader has the responsibility of preselling the product to the household. The cereal and automobile industries are good examples of pull philosophies in operation.

Channel amalgamation is a second significant trend. amalgamation is associate with the emergence of large manufacturers and retailers in many industries. This emergence has brought about the decline of selected wholesalers and other intermediaries operating between the manufacturer and the retailer.

The home furnishing industry has been traditionally composed of many small furniture producers and thousands of small retailers. Given his channel composition, highly profitable intermediaries performed many significant functions. Recently, however, giant firms like Armstrong Cork and Weyerhauser have extended their product lines into home furnishings. On the retail side, national and regional firms, such as Levitz and RB Furniture, have assumed growing prominence. Where does this put the intermediary? Since the industry is changing all channel members must adjust. The intermediaries must redefine the services they render to both the manufacturers and the retailers.

Low margin retailing is a trend that has been going on for some time now. Firs such as K-Mart have adopted a strategy of accepting a lower price per item sold in order to gain profits through higher volume sales. The advent of self-service has helped lower costs and hence kept prices attractive. Low margin retailing has forced most small independents to stress their nonprice competitive advantages and stimulated the growth of retailer-and wholesaler-dominated associations.

Stock philosophy has completed a fully cycle from the general store to retailer specialization to *scrambled merchandising*. The latter term describes competition between different *types* of retail outlets marketing similar goods. A food store such as Safeway or A & P is now marketing housewares, nonprescription drugs, and clothing, as well as food. The variety of products marketed suggests that the food store is competing with retailers within and outside the food business. In terestingly enough, a most recent retailing phenomenon is the emergence of the boutique. This may seem to represent a movement back to specialization, but it should be noted that the boutiques prosper best when surrounded by a variety of other retailers, such as the situation found in major shopping malls. All members of the distribution channel need to continually monitor the strategic implications of these retailing changes.

The *location* of retailing establishments has changed drastically in the last decade. The decline of downtown shopping areas and the growth of shopping centers is obvious, but other trends are also in various stages of development. More and more outlets are moving into or near the larger office buildings, industrial parks, and apartment complexes. This development is a response to people who want to spend less time and effort shopping for certain items-particularly convenience goods. Furthermore, an increasing percentage of retail volume is done outside the store. The popularity of catalog shopping may be the prelude to buying through means of a minicomputer in the home.

Leasing and *credit* availability have also facilitated channel trends. Tax and capital advantages have led many industrial firms to leasing on a massive scale. Many airlines, in fact, lease their aircraft from commercial banks. Although leasing in nonhousehold markets is well developed, observers also anticipate substantial growth in consumer leasing in the years ahead. Credit availability and arrangements have stimulated all institutions in the channel by making it easier for buyers to engage in consumption activities.

Channel strategy involves the goal of

attaining an optimal distributive structure through which products and services may flow. A channel may have any number of members, and control will usually reside with the firm possessing the greatest economic power. Given this background, the next section will examine the actual physical movement of products from the manufacturer to the consumer.

Physical distribution strategy

Given a specified level of customer service and an existing channel structure, the goal of physical distribution strategy is to minimize the cost involved in physically moving and storing the product from its production point to the point where it is ultimately purchased.

1. Determining inventory dispersion
2. Determining g the level of inventory
3. Selecting a mode(s) of transportation

Unfortunately, these tasks have often been viewed as a group of unrelated activities. Managerial responsibility for them as often been assigned to areas in the firm that may have incongruent goals. The ultimate result of this fragmented approach is the suboptimization of overall physical distribution goals. It is irrational, for instance, to focus on reducing transportation costs when to do so has the effect of increasing the cost of carrying inventory by an increment greater than the amount saved.

Inventory dispersion: The strategic decision here is to what extent does the firm want to centralize its inventory or disperse it throughout the market. If the firm is the marketer of Winston cigarettes, it may want its product available within an arm's length of consumption. On the other hand, if the firm is marketing steamshovels, it would be ludicrous for it to have the product available on every corner. As a matter of fact, for some products, it is advisable to maintain *no* inventory and simply produce the item when an order is received. The no inventory policy is particularly appropriate when the product is customized to the needs of the customer.

What are the factors that should be considered in determining inventory dispersion? First, and foremost, is demand or market considerations coupled with what competitors are doing. These factors, in turn, must be balanced against cost variables. Various mathematical models are available to help guide this strategic decision.

Inventory size: Determining optimal inventory size is a natural extention of the dispersion decision. Inventory control represents a trade off between the cost of carrying inventory versus the cost of being out of stock. If a firm could afford to be solely concerned with serving customers, it would make sure that it always had ample inventory available to satisfy potential customers' orders. Higher service levels, however, require larger inventories, which in turn lead to high storage costs, capital cost, taxes and insurance, possible deterioration and obsolescence, and losses if prices decline. Conversely, smaller inventory levels can lead to frequent order processing, high handling charges, loss of quantity discounts, losses if prices increase, and possible out of stock, with resulting customer dissatisfaction.

Every student has probably experienced something like the following situation. The semester begins and you go over to the bookstore to purchase your texts. Unfortunately, you discover that *Marketing And Environmental perspective* has been sold out and another shipment will not be in for three weeks. After exhibiting various levels of disgust toward the bookstore and may be even toward the authors of the text, you resign yourself to being without the book for the beginning of the course. Where did the bookstore go wrong? Obviously, they underestimated the demand for your marketing book and there are costs to them as a result. On the other hand. If they had over estimated demand they would be left with an excess inventory and its associated costs. Thus, the bookstore tries to correctly guess the correct number of texts to order to minimize the aforementioned costs.

These tradeoffs make the timing of inventory purchases critical. Guidelines must be established so that reordering of stock automatically takes place when prescribed inventory levels are reached. Most companies maintain a basic inventory at al times, along with a "safety stock" as a hedge against variability of lead order time. Quantitative relationships can ordinarily be developed to provide insight as to appropriate reorder points and economic order quantities.

Transportation modes: In addition to inventory strategy, physical distribution also involves selecting modes of transportation. Basically there are five alternatives that can be used: railroads, motor carriers, water carriers, pipelines, and airlines. Excluding air freight which accounts for less than 1 percent of all shipments, Figure 6.8 shows the relative importance of the four major modes of transportation in terms of intercity ton-miles hauled by each during the period 1940-1971.

Railroads are the leading mode, followed by pipelines, motor carriers, and water carriers. The attractiveness of the railroads is their ability to haul bulk products and raw materials relatively inexpensively and quickly to almost any point in the United States.

The motor carrier industry, which has shown dramatic growth in the past ten years, provides fast and consistent service for both large and small shipments. Although it cannot ordinarily haul bulk products as inexpensively as the railroads, it frequently can provide a cost advantage for manufactured products. As a result, in the early 1970s truckers received revenue of five times the cents per ton-mile than the railroads.

Water carriers, particularly barge lines that operate on the inland waterways, concentrate on bulk commodities. Ocean-going ships operate on the Great Lakes and international waters. In 1971 domestic water billings amounted to $1.37 billion, and the international freight bill was more than $4.3 billion.

Many people overlook pipelines as a major means of transportation, but they are second only to railroads in number of ton-miles transported. Pipelines are the most efficient conveyors of oil products and natural gas with average revenue per ton-mile being less than 3 cents. Basically, oil pipelines haul two types of commodities-crude oil and refined products such as gasoline and kerosene. A third area of increasing importance is slurry pipelines. They transport groundup products, such as coal, in a water suspension.

The last mode of transportation is air freight. Growth has been dramatic, as evidenced by an increase of almost 2.5 billion ton-miles flown in the last decade. Yet, air freight still only accounts for less than 1 percent of total ton-miles transported. Air freight, because of its relatively high cost, is used primarily for the shipment of very valuable or highly perishable products.

The complex decisions involved in selecting a given mode have made transportation a specialized field in itself. Strategically, the firm should select the mode(s) that best matches transport costs and services with customer requirements. If speed, for example, is the essential need of the buyer, then air freight is the appropriate mode, assuming the buyer is willing to bear the cost.

Organization: The area of physical distribution is

receiving great attention today. This interest is a direct result of the increasing complexity and importance of the activity.

Organizationally, physical distribution is positioned in various departments, such as marketing, production, and traffic. The fact that physical distribution has no common home reinforces our knowledge that it is a multifaceted activity. The importance of the activity to many firms has resulted in the creation of a separate physical distribution department at the same level as marketing, production, an other departments. If a high level of customer service is required and physical flows are an important element in the firm's overall success, a separate unit may be justifiable.

The macro environment and distribution strategy

As with the other three elements of the marketing mix, distribution strategy is influenced by forces *outside* the firm. A company must continually monitor changes in the macro environment and assess their impact on distribution strategy.

Sociocultural, legal, and *competitive* force are relevant in the distribution of Coors beer in the eastern half of the United States Coors is the nation's fourth largest selling beer, despite being widely distributed in only eleven western states. The beer's light, smooth taste, coupled with its limited geographical distribution, have created a "Coors mystique" among beer drinkers outside the west. Coors' ability to totally control its distribution channels is slipping as a result of a

Supreme Court ruling that the company could not prohibit sales to the other 39 states. as a consequence, wholesalers and retailers are now buying the beer in western states and transporting it eastward. The "Coors mystique" and the few places it is available outside the west have allowed selected retailers to charge astronomical prices for the beer. philadelphia distributor Paul Lipschutz, for example, began importing the beer and lines formed even though the price was $12.50 a case. Coors, distributors, and retailers will be carefully monitoring the public to see if the increased availability of the beer will hurt the "Coors mystique."

Coordinating the marketing mix

An organization must be able to adjust these elements for existing and new products periodically if it wants to have a successful marketing effort.

While each of the four mix elements requires a specific strategy, each depends on and affects the others. Changes in a product, for example, are likely to suggest adjustments in promotion strategy. As the product passes through the introductory, growth, maturity, and decline stages, the marketing mix should change.

This chapter has examined promotion and distribution strategy-two of the four elements of the marketing mix. Promotion strategy is the means by which the organization communicates with the marketplace. Marketing communications flow from a source through a channel to a receiver. The goal of promotion is to inform, persuade, and remind consumers about all relevant aspects of the firm's offering.

The marketer has a number of promotional tools to select from. The marketer may choose various combinations of advertising, personal selling, sales promotion, packaging, branding, public relations, and publicity. Generally, the two most significant elements in promotion strategy are advertising and personal selling.

Advertising is the impersonal communication of ideas, goods, or services to a mass audience by an identified paying sponsor. The ultimate objective of most advertising is to hasten the adoption or ensure repeat purchases of a product or service. Determining the appropriate copy and media are strategic advertising decisions. Market characteristics, product attributes, and cost are important considerations in making these decisions. The creative and technical aspects of advertising often result in firms using the services of advertising agencies.

Personal selling, in contrast to advertising, enables the firm to approach the market on a more selective basis and benefit from one-to-one interaction. Various estimates suggest that 10 percent of the nation's labor force may be engaged in this activity. Today's professional salespersons are attuned to their customers' needs and familiar with the intricate attributes of their products and services.

Although each of the promotion techniques is separate and distinct, an effective promotion strategy orchestrates the elements into a coordinated communications effort. The macro environment establishes constraints as well as opportunities in formulating promotion strategy.

Distribution strategy consists of getting the product to the customer when and where he or she wants it. The broad strategic decisions can be divided into (a) the channels through which products flow, and (b) the physical movement of products through the channel.

Distribution channels encompass all of the institutions involved in product flow from point of manufacture to point of final purchase. Middlemen such as wholesalers, retailers, and agents help facilitate the flow. Generally one of the institutions in the channel assumes the leadership in influencing channel decisions. Although channels represent an aggregation of separate firms, the movement toward vertical channel systems has reduced interfirm conflicts and often led to goal congruence among the participants. Significant channel trends in recent years include the adoption of the pull philosophy, channel amalgamation, low margin retailing variable stock philosophy, location changes, and the popularity of leasing and credit.

The strategic task of physical distribution may be divided into three areas: (1) determining inventory dispersion; (2) determining the level of inventory; and (3) selecting a mode of transportation. Inventory dispersion is to what extent a firm wants to centralize its inventory or disperse it throughout the market. Inventory level decisions represent a tradeoff between the cost of carrying inventory versus the cost of being out of stock. Transportation modes may be selected from rail, motor water, pipeline, and air carriers. The complexity and importance of physical distribution has led to debates on where in the organization this activity should be located.

A successful distribution strategy coordinates all of the relevant elements into a systematized effort. As with promotion strategy, decisions concerning this mix element are influenced by the macro environment.

5 The Market Target and Promotion Appeal

Successful promotional strategy usually requires that the target of the effort be carefully defined in order to isolate those individuals who are potentially receptive to the promotional message. This reduces waste by saving dollars that would have been spent trying to persuade those who cannot be persuaded. More importantly, defining the target figuratively groups people into a collective "one", which provides a concrete basis for developing effective communication in accordance with the tenets of sound communication theory. Furthermore, characteristics of the target group help in design and implementation of specific facets of promotional strategy.

The market target

Obviously, a market is composed of people with needs to satisfy, but such people must also be financially able to buy our product and be willing to do so, given the proper incentive. How do we identify and isolate such people? There are two basic approaches: (1) product differentiation and (2) market segmentation. Both marketing management and promotion management are concerned with this task, and the approach chosen usually reflects total marketing strategy of which promotion is a part.

Product differentiation

The company that chooses to follow a policy of product differentiation views the total market for a product as one fairly homogeneous unit. Such a firm takes the position that there is a market for facial tissues, or ball-point pens, or refrigerators, or whatever, and that the company can generate sales within the total market simply by making its product a little different from those of its competitors. The management of such firms does not expect to capture the entire market. Rather, it simply believes that there will be enough people across the entire range of the market who could be convinced of the merits of the product to justify production.

Usually firms that adopt a policy of product differentiation are production oriented; that is, they are less concerned with marketing than they are with production. They may spend less time analyzing the consumer and devote more attention to the problems of production-more or less assuming that the product will sell in sufficient quantities to justify its existence.

Except for certain products such as wheat, natural gas, and other products of a "basic" nature, product differentiation as a strategy is risky in the volatile marketplace of contemporary business. The total market for most products today is simply too heterogeneous to be considered as a single unit. The needs of people and their reasons for buying, both real and imaginary, are so diversified that a single product tossed at the total market will usually find few catchers. A notable exception is perhaps the Morton Salt Company, which is probably oriented to a product differentiation policy. "When it rains it pours" has successfully distinguished the company's product from those of its competitors in the total salt market for many years.

Market segmentation

The other approach to defining a market target is much more common today. Some form of market segmentation is probably used by a majority of manufacturers. I is simply dividing the total market into segments, each of which consist of people with homogeneous characteristics with respect to purchase behavior. Thus, instead of saying there is one market for facial tissues, or ball-point pens, or refrigerators, the firm whose strategy is market segmentation would say there are several markets for each of these products and that the markets are delineated by certain common characteristics of people that are unique to their respective groups.

The policy is consumer oriented, and is therefore consistent with current marketing theory. In essence, its use requires analyzing consumers to determine the kind of product wanted and possible reasons for buying it and then creating a product accordingly. Promotion's part in the process is to convince the people in the appropriate segment(s) that the product is just what they want.

Market segmentation results in a much more precisely defined target than does product differentiation. The firm using the latter strategy simply thrown its product up for grabs and hopes there will be some takers, but the firm using market segmentation zeros in on a specific target. Most companies design and promote variations of a product for each of several different market segments. Procter and Gamble for example, promotes Crest toothpaste to a market segment consisting of families who are concerned about tooth decay problems of their children and promotes Gleam to a different segment. Lever Brothers reaches different market segments with Aim and Close-up as does Colgate-Palmolive with Colgate and Ultra Brite. Automobile manufactures also appeal to many different market segments with the many models and styles of their products.

The significance of market segmentation to promotion is at least twofold: (1) it provides the best answers to the question of why people might want to buy the product; and (2) it identifies potential receivers of the promotion message, thereby suggesting additional clues for developing effective·communication. In fact, the importance of market segmentation to promotion is of sufficient magnitude as to justify and examination of the strategy in some depth.

Positioning the product

Essential to approaching the problem of segmenting the market is the proper positioning of the product in the market. A product's position refers to the way it is perceived vis-a-vis products of competitors or other products in the company's product mix. It is extremely important that the product be positioned properly. Avis could not successfully position itself against Hertz and changed its position to "Number 2." And 7-Up had to change its position from that of a direct competitor of Coca-Cola and Pepsi-Cola to a different drink-the "Un-cola." Products positioning requires that the firm determine the niche in the array of product offerings that is appropriate for the product in question. It means that the firm must decide on the source from which it intends to carve its market share.

Criteria used for market segmenting

When a criterion is used for segmenting the market, it is not to criterion itself that is the fact that the people identified by that criterion exhibit similar behaviour with respect to their purchases. When age is used as a criterion for segmentation, for example, it is not the fact that certain people are teenagers that is important, but rather that most teenagers display similar patterns in their purchase behaviour. Markets are usually segmented by using combination of several criteria. Although it is not possible to identify all the criteria used for segmenting markets, it is useful to discus briefly some of the more commonly used bases. They can be divided conveniently into three groups. (1) demographic (2) sociological, and (3) psychographic.

Demographic: An obvious demographic factor that serves to delineate separate market segments for some products is sex. Certain products are solely for women, and other are designed for men. Yet with the changing values and "unisex" movement is reflected in may items of clothing, sporting equipment, jewelry, and other product categories. "For some products, the division is not appropriate, but in many cases in an automatic segmenting factor.

Another common basis for segmentation is age. The wants and needs of people vary among different age groups. In addition, even when there is little difference among age groups with respect to products wanted, it is often necessary to use be specially adapted, different media used, and so on. However because of the youth orientation that seems to prevail in our society today, promotion techniques with the youthful tone may be more effective with older groups that they once were. Pepsi-Cola's" for those who think young" slogan of a few years ago reflects a recognition of this phenomenon. Who in contemporary society does not want to "think Younger".

On the other hand, the traditional division of people into groups defined as children, teens, young married, and adults may fail to represent a growing and increasingly important segment or society-the elderly. The category "adults" makes no distinction between elderly consumers and other adults. And, yet, it is quite probable that the elderly consumes and other adults. And, yet, it is quite probable that the elderly differ from other adults with respect tot he mass media to which they expose themselves, the way they learn, and perhaps their influenceability.

An important basis for segmenting the market is *family life cycle*. The term refers to the stages of family life through which most people go. Typical categories composing the family life cycle include bachelors, young marrieds with no children, young marrieds with children, older marrieds with dependent children at home, the "empty nest," and older singles. As with all segmenting factors, the stages so delineated designate people whose wants, needs, and purchase behaviour are similar within each stage and different among stages.

Other demographic criteria useful for segmenting the market for some products include *income, education, occupation, race religion nationality*, and population distribution. A person's total income determines the amount of disposable income and discretionary buying power availably for spending. The amount of such income this has a bearing on the type, quality, and quantity of product demanded Education likewise influences purchase behaviour. Generally speaking, more education creates more discerning consumers with respect to both product characteristics and promotion messages. People in certain occupations provide markets for some products not for others. Race, religion, and nationally can all be identified with certain cultural characteristics that have an influence on the kinds of products purchased and the responses to promotional efforts. And the distribution of population is a key factor in the designation of geographic market segments.

Sociological: Markets may also be segmented on the basis of such cultural and social factors as regional tastes and customs, organizational behaviour guidelines, behavioural influences at various school levels, leisure activities, social class, and other people in the Southwest for example comprise an especially strong market segment for various types of Mexican foods and certain styles of clothing. New England and the Deep South are other examples of regions with unique cultural characteristics that influence purchase behaviour. Organizations such as Chambers of Commerce, labour unions, faternities and sororities, youth organizations such as Little League, Girl and Boy Scouts, DeMolay, and others prescribe certain kinds of behaviour that are reflected in purchases.

Different behaviour sanctions identified at each level of school suggest possible market segments. Leisure activities create a significant and growing market segment for certain types of products. And social class must not be ignored. Even though the lines between social classes in. He United States are somewhat blurred, certain kinds of purchase behaviour are associated with each class.

Market can also be segmented according to

the degree to which individuals use a particular product. Thus segments could be defined as consisting of heavy users, light users, or nonusers. The particular criterion can be quite significant to promotional strategy because the question often arises as to whether it is more profitable to concentrate promotional efforts on those people who are already favourably inclined toward the product or on those who are not presently using it. And sometimes it may be wise to try to change light users to heavy users. The appropriate strategy depends upon the nature of the situation.

Psychographic: Among the more recent approaches for solving the difficult problems of effectively segmenting the market is one that builds on the concept of psychographics-the study of personality traits of individuals. The rationale underlying the approach, which has been referred to as life-style segmentation, is that a better understanding of customers results in more effective communication and marketing efforts. "It deals, essentially, with the attitudes, feelings, and opinions of people keting efforts. :It deals, essentially, with the attitudes, feelings, and opinions of people as they are reflected in behaviour patterns. Psychographics thus adds another dimension to demographics in defining the market target. The research associated with it is "intended to place consumers on psychological-as distinguished from demographic-dimensions. For example a market segment might not be defined simply as middle-aged office workers, but as party-going middle-aged office workers.

Thus the use of certain products can sometimes be identified with particular behaviour patterns, and he market can be segmented accordingly. One study showed that the heavy user of eye makeup was an entirely different kind of person than the heavy user of shortening.

Perplexing aspects

Market segmentation is perhaps the best approach available for defining market targets, but it is not a panacea. For one thing, any person may fit into several different market segments during the week, or even a day, because of situations requiring the use of a different product. Thc same person who uses a compact car for city driving may use a larger car for highway travel. Even more confusing is the fact that different situations may require the use of different brands of the same generic product. The Macho man may buy "Old Rotgut" for his everyday highballs, but when he gives a cocktail party for his boss and influential friends, he buys "Wild turkey." This is also a reflection of role theory. It has been suggested that under such conditions a viable approach to market segmentation is to think in terms of the conditions under which the product will be used.

A related problem is that of selecting the appropriate segmentation variable. Because there are so many variables, it is often difficult to know which is most relevant to the purpose. Furthermore, each situation is unique.

In a study based on the significance of each of four segmentation variables income, social class, age, and family life cycle-it was found that a variable significant in one product/market context may not be significant in another. Thus, income might be used effectively to segment the market for off-brands of soft drinks, but age, social class, peer pressure, or something else may be more appropriately used in connection with nationally known brands.

Market sementation is also aptly used in retailing. Typically, majority of shoppers attracted to a particular retail store are a fairly homogeneous group with respect to certain variables associated with their purchase behaviour. Indeed, the most successful retailers attempt to identify the most promising of such groups on the basis of appropriate segmentation variables and gear their operation accordingly. It is significant, however, that segmentation studies for one type of retailer do not necessarily provide information relevant to other types.

The problem of market segmentation is also magnified by the fact that often the customer who purchases the product is not the decision maker. Under these circumstances, the question of who really is the market target for promotional effort becomes confusing. The proper target, of course, is the person who decides whether to buy or not to buy-not necessarily the one who actually makes the purchase in store, or even the one who uses the product. But it is sometimes difficult to know who that person is.

For example, who decides on the brand of coffee to buy-the husband of the wife? A price difference among brands may be the decision criterion by consensus. But if the price of most major brands of coffee is about the same, brand choice is determined on the basis of something else-by someone. Suppose a husband says to his wife, "Pick up a package of razor blades when you are in the store"; or the wife says to her husband, "Get me some panty hose when you do the shopping today." In either of these cases, the customer is probably not the user and may or may not be the decision maker with respect to brands.

It is not by accident that cereals are usually placed on lower shelves in supermarkets. Nor is it unusual for a parent to find a box of "Poopsie Woopsies" in the grocery cart at the checkout stand. When this happens, the typical scene is that the parent chastizes the child for picking up the box but buys it anyhow. So, who was the logical target for promotional effort, the customer or the child?

Opportunity for effective promotion

Among the numerous problems associated with developing a promotional strategy is that of determining the relative potential for success of a particular product/market effort. Resolving the issue would probably be done concurrently with the task of segmenting the market. The problem is that all products re not equally promotable, nor are all markets equally persuadable. Certain characteristics of each product and market have a bearing on the possible effectiveness of a promotional strategy. If an analysis of such characteristics indicates futility for the proposed effort, perhaps it should either be abandoned or at least be given relatively less support than other more promising possibilities.

Product characteristics

The classic codification of conditions associated with a product that increase the probability of success in its promotion was suggested by Neil H. Borden a number of years ago. Despite the passage of time, the "laws" paraphrased below still stand. There is a greater chance for success in advertising a product if:

1. There is a favorable primary demand for the product.
2. The product can be effectively differentiated from competing products.
3. There are hidden qualities in the product that are important to the consumer.
4. There are strong emotional buying motives with respect to the product.
5. There are sufficient funds to support the amount of advertising necessary for effectiveness.

Primary demand

The demand for the generic product is primary demand. If the demand is favourable for the generic product, advertising will be easier and more effective. If there is no existing demand for the product, there certainly is no existing demand for a particular brand of the product; and under such conditions a major focus of the promotional effort must be on stimulating primary demand. Such advertising would benefit competitors as well as the firm initiating the effort.

This is not to say that a firm should never engage in primary demand advertising. Sometimes it is necessary, as was the case when microwave ovens first appeared on the market. Any new product whose use would result in a major change in living habits will likely require some degree of primary demand advertising. But emphasis on the generic product tends to dilute the effectiveness of brand advertising.

Differentiation

It would be extremely difficult to advertise a product that could not be differentiated from competing products. What could be said about the product? An extension of this notion is suggested in Borden's third condition.

Hidden qualities: If there are hidden qualities in the product, there is something to talk about in the advertising that is not obvious to the consume but makes the product different from other brands. Toothpastes, for example, are advertised as having special ingredients to make teeth white or to prevent cavities; soap have special cleansing agents; and pain relievers are made with special formulas.

Emotional motives

Finally a product is more advertisable if there are strong emotional reasons for buying it. This is true partly because emotion plays a large part in the purchase of many products, and partly because it is often easier to appeal to emotion than to rationality.

If the foregoing conditions exist, there is a greater opportunity for effective advertising than if they are not present. The absence of any one or all does not mean the product should not be advertised; it simply means that the chances for success are reduced.

Market characteristics

In this and earlier chapters, we have discussed factors influencing the market's existence, its characterization, and its delineation if it does exist. However, another characteristic of the market, could have a more direct bearing on the effectiveness of a particular promotional strategy. This characteristic is product acceptance.

People in a market may vary in the degree to which they have accepted a product. In the market for most products there will be some people who have been using the product for quite some time because they began using it when it was first introduced. Others will be trying it for the first time, and still others will not have even considered using it. This principle is illustrated very clearly in Everett Rogers' adopter categories for new products.

Roges' five categories of adopters were based on the rapidity with which people adopt innovations: Innovators, 2.5 percent of the people; early adopters, 13.5 percent; early majority, 34 percent; late majority, 34 percent; and laggards, 16 percent. Thumbnail descriptions of the people in each category portray innovators as venturesome risk-takers, early adopters as respectable people having opinion leadership, early majority as deliberate in their actions and as followers but seldom leaders, late majority as skeptical and requiring pressure of peers for adoption, and laggards as traditional with no opinion leadership who probably do not adopt the product until after it has been superseded by another.

Rogers' work dealt with the adoption and diffusion of innovations, but it is evident that at any given time ate a company has introduced a new product there will be at least two adopter categories of people in the market. The significance of the notion is that there may be varying degrees of opportunity for successful promotion, depending somewhat upon the degree to which the product has been accepted. Furthermore, the number of people in each category will have a bearing on the type of promotional effort that will be most productive.

The promotion appeal

Once the market target has been defined and it has been determined that there is an opportunity for effective promotion, there arises the problem of determining the appropriate appeal. The promotion appeal, although difficult to define except in the abstract, is often the major reason for success or failure in a particular promotion effort.

The appeal is the basic idea that forms the core of a promotional message. It provides the foundation guideline for constructing the message. In essence, it is the source of persuasiveness, if such exists, in the promotional effort.

Choosing the appeal is not as formidable a task as it might seem-if the necessary homework has been done. As a matter of fact, much of the discussion so are in this book reflects the kind of analysis needed for the determination of an effective appeal. What is required is a through understanding of those who make up the target of the proposed efforts. Persons with a good deal of experience in promotional activity may rely on instinct for ideas, but such instinct is usually the result of numerous experiences with structured formal research. In any event, favourable responses to promotion messages can usually be obtained only if the appeal has been developed with the intended audience in ming. Furthermore, visualizing this audience by such techniques as those embodied in the field of psychographics assists in the development of effective communication.

Buying motives, determined by a thorough analysis of the market segment, serve as the point of orientation for establishing the promotion appeal. The buying motive usually suggests the promotion appeal since the intended audience can only be persuaded if it is convinced that the product answers perceived needs. Therefore, it is often convenient to identify promotion appeals in terms of buying motives. Appeals referred to as price, dependability, prestige, or sex, for example, reflect their orientation to their respective buying motives. This is true whether the subject of the effort is a product, service, or idea. The appeals used in promoting political candidates or social causes, for example, are only effective to the extent that they reflect reasons people might have for "buying" them. The same is true for corporate advertising; the business whose promotion objective is to improve its corporate acceptability should use appeals that reflect reasons people could have for believing it is socially responsible, reasons to "buy" the ideas presented in the message.

A necessary complement to the consideration of buying motives in developing the promotion appeal is an analysis of the characteristics of the product, service, or idea involved. What is there about the product that would satisfy the needs that give rise to the buying motive? It must be remembered that a typical product has both tangible and intangible characteristics, any of which might fulfill the needs of certain people. The promotional strategist must identify those particular product characteristics that relate to the buying motives as determined, whether they are biogenic or psychogenic motives. The appeal can then be developed accordingly. Thus if the reason for buying the product is to impress the opposite sex, a sex appeal can be used whereby those characteristics of the product that would enhance effectiveness in this regard would be extolled. If, on the other hand, consumers are looking for durability in a particular product, those characteristics that indicate this feature should be included in the implementation of the appeal. And so on.

Promotion appeals can be stated in positive or negative terms. Positive appeals emphasize the benefits to be obtained from using the product or accepting the idea; negative appeals warn people of the disadvantages of not doing so. We are urged, for example, to use Camay for a sensuous bath feel but Deial to avoid offending others-Don't you wish everyone did?" In any case, the reference is always to the benefits associated with the product.

Generally speaking, positive appeals are more effective than negative appeals, but there are some products and product categories for which negative appeals are quite effective. The myriad personal care products-deodorants mouthwashes, lotions, creams, perfumes, colognes-are often promoted with the focus on the undesirable situation we would be in if we failed to use them. Both kinds of appeals are used in promoting life insurance. If the emphasis is on insurance as investment for college educations or retirement, the appeal is positive. But playing up disaster that befalls a family without insurance when the breadwinner suddenly dies is a negative appeal. The latter is an example of the use of a fear appeal. Although the effectiveness of fear appeals has been debated over the years, the fact that it is used successfully in some promotional situations would seem to attest to its usefulness.

Since it is unusual for a specific product to be equally acceptable to everyone, it is usually necessary for promotional strategists to identify specific market targets. Not only does this isolate groups of people whose buying motives are similar, but it also provides a common ground that makes communication easier and more effective. There are two ways to accomplish this: product differentiation and market segmentation.

Product differentiation is a policy by means of which the firm hopes to tap a portion of the total range of the market. Market segmentation, on the other hand, entails dividing the total market into smaller segments, each of which is composed of people with similar characteristics with respect to their purchase behaviour. Criteria useful for segmenting the market can be divided into three groups: demographic, sociological, and psychographic. Associated with market segmentation is the problem of positioning the product. This is establishing the product in the market in its proper niche-the way it will likely be perceived relative to competitive products and to other products in the company's line.

Opportunities for successful promotion vary. Certain conditions associated with the product and the market are significant in this regard. A favourable primary demand for the product, distinguishing characteristics, and the possibility of using emotional appeals increase the chances for success, as does the degree to which people in the market have adopted the product.

The promotion appeal is the theme of the message. It is the way the product is interpreted to the intended audience, and it is based on buying motives. In fact, the appeal is often identified by the buying motives that suggested it.

6 Promotion and the Communication Process

We communicate in many ways. We speak, write, whistle, raise our eyebrows, lift our arms, shake our heads, grunt, groan, cry, yawn, clear our throats, or leave the room. It is not possible to conceive of any environment existing in the absence of communication in many forms.

On the other hand, there are many times when we try to communicate but are unable to do so. How many times have you talked with someone who obviously did not hear what you were saying? You could tell that your conversational partner was not listening because you could almost see his or her mind working on what to say when you stopped talking. The response, then, confirmed your observation.

There are also times when we think we have communicated only to find that the idea we thought we were conveying was not perceived by our listener. We were misunderstood, and communication did not take place

Because promotion is communication, we must understand the communication process to understand effective promotion.

The concept of communication

The term communication stems from the Latin, communis, which means common. Our purpose in communicating is to establish something in common with another person or persons. We do this by imparting information, knowledge, thoughts, and opinions to those with whom we wish to establish the relationship.

It is often argued that in some instances we are simply attempting to inform, while in other cases we are trying to persuade. Others suggest that all communication is an attempt to persuade in some way-if only to accept the statements we make in any event, effective promotion requires persuasive communication.

Communication takes place when those with whom we are attempting to communicate attach a meaning to the message that is similar to the meaning we are trying to convey. This similarity of interpretation is necessary in all communication situations, but it is particularly significant in promotion because mass communication is often required.

A communication model

Communication literature is repiete with models of the communication process. The models are similar with respect to the elements they contain, however, they may differ in terminology, in the exact number of items included, and in the precise interpretation of relationships and effects.

The following elements are common in all communication situations and in most models; source, message, encoding, channels, decoding, receiver, noise, and feedback. For purposes of this discussion, encoding and decoding will be expressed as activities, rather than as people or things.

It is necessary to understand each element and its relationship to the others in order to develop an effective promotional effort.

Source

The source is the originator of the message. The source may be an individual, such as salesperson talking to a customer, a minister preaching to a congregation, or a candidate for political office expounding to an audience. The source may also be an organization such as a business, a charitable institution, or a government agency. Each of these institutions originates countless messages about products, services, and ideas that it is trying to promote to appropriate targets.

The receiver may or may not be aware of the source's identity. In a conversation between two people, of course, each knows the other as the source of the message. In an advertisement the source is identified in the message.

The source, however, is not always recognized. Sometimes receivers confuse the source with the vehicle of transmission-the newspaper or the radio, for example. You have no doubt heard such expressions as, "The paper says it's going to rain today"; or "According to the radio, the stock market was down yesterday". In these cases, the source is not the newspaper or the radio; it is some other institution or individual using the newspaper or the radio as the channel or transmission.

Confusion also arises when the person presenting the message is mistaken for the source. This frequently happens when well-known personalities such as athletes or entertainers present the commercials. Again, the source is not the individual reading the message, it is the business whose product is being advertised. Sometimes such mistaken identity provides pseudocredibility to the real source and thereby aids in the reception and acceptance of the message.

This latter notion suggests that the source's credibility in the eyes of the receiver is a significant factor in communication. Clearly, one is more likely to believe what is said if the source is considered reliable than if it is suspect.

Message

The message might be thought of as an idea in transmittable form. The message originates in the source, and its content is suggested by circumstances that gave rise to the idea to the first place . However, its form is determined by conditions and forces affecting perception and receptivity of the message once it has been transmitted . Designing the form is the task of encoding.

A significant step in promotion is determining the appropriate idea to communicate. The relevancy of the intended message determines whether or not communication takes place. Often, people are not aware of messages unrelated to their interests. They "tune out" such messages, and communication does not occur.

Therefore, the promotional strategist must be as certain as possible that the message is right for the purpose audience. A careful and thorough analysis of the individuals or groups who make up the target audience puts the strategist in a better position to understand what the communication objectives must be and what ideas should be communicated to produce the desired effect. After content is determined, it is necessary to put it into communicable form-to encode it into message.

Encoding

The purpose in communication is to transmit an idea. The originator of the idea hopes to recreate in the receiver's mind precisely the same thing he or she has in mind. "When we communicate, we are trying to establish a commonness' with someone". Because we experience so much misunderstanding in communication situations, we know that this commonness is often difficult to establish.

Encoding is the process of putting the message into a form that can be transmitted, received, and understood by the receiver. This form is usually a written or spoken language, although it does not have to be. For example, the symbols used on street and highway signs and the shape of the signs. Indicate very clearly the intended message, without the use of language. The important point is that the devices used in the encoding process must mean the same thing to both source and receiver; otherwise communication will not take place.

Encoding is complicated by the fact that one word often has different meanings and shades of meanings. Furthermore, since no two people ever have the same experiences, it is not likely that perfect communication between sender and receiver is ever achieved.

One way to minimize communication error, assuming that the message's content has been properly determined, is to exercise some degree of empathy while encoding the message. An encoder who sees the communication situation through the receiver's eyes is more likely to use the language, signs, and symbols that will be meaningful to the receiver and convey the idea. The same message, for example, might be encoded one way if it were being transmitted to a professional engineer and an entirely different way if the target were a high school student.

Market segmentation, breaking the market into smaller homogeneous group, serves a number of purposes in marketing. Its primary significance in promotion is related to the encoding process as it must be applied in mass communication. The receivers in a mass audience must be considered as a collective "one". The only way that this is possible is to segment the audience into homogeneous groups and then communicate with each group as if the people in the group were one receiver.

External encoder: The source is always the originator but not always the encoder. In some situations the source may not be qualified to encode the message in transmittable form or in a form what would be accepted and understood by the receiver. The receiver may have insufficient knowledge or the source may lack the ability to encode the message. It is common for such organizations as advertising agencies, media personnel, and public relations agencies to act as encodes of messages aimed at mass audiences. It is also quite common for senior salespeople and sales organizations to encode messages conceived by sales managers to be delivered by new salespeople.

Channels

The channel is the link between the source and the receiver-the means by which the message is transmitted. The channel may be the human voice in personal selling situations; it may be the printed word in magazine and newspaper advertising; it may be the spoken work on radio or television; or, it may be something else or a combination of many things.

The wise choice of communication channels is highly complex. Yet too often sources such as advertisers, politicians, and social-cause advocates assume that because the idea is good it is only necessary to see that it is transmitted to the receiver by some expedient means. Such sources are often surprised by the poor results produced from this tactic.

Moreover, it is not usual for the secondary channel to have a greater impact on the receiver than does the primary channel. If such impact reinforces the message being transmitted, the effect is good. When a after speaks to his son and says, "I want you to tell me where you were last night", and punctuates his words with a shaking of his fist and a threatening look, the intended message comes through loud and clear.

On the other hand, the secondary channels may distort the intended message to the extent that it is ineffective or even negated. For example, a meek salesperson may be selling a good product and have a good message; but making the sales presentation in an apologetic manner showing a complete lack of confidence negates the intended message. The secondary channels. The intended message in the primary channel, which points out the favorable aspects of the product, will be completely overshadowed by the message in the secondary channel, which says that the salesperson does not really believe in the product.

Secondary channels are not restricted to face-to-face situations, but are also significant in mass communication. Certain magazines are considered more prestigious than others, and their prestige will act as a secondary channel by adding impact to the message placed in them-impact that would not be present if the message were placed in other magazines. In a single magazine the size and style of type used in an advertisement will act as a secondary channel. The positioning of messages, both in print media and in broadcast media, creates secondary channels. Advertisers should very carefully consider the television programs with which they may be identified; the association itself could be a secondary channel.

Noise

In addition to the difficulties posed by multiple channels of transmission, the communicator is always faced with the problem of noise. Noise in this sense refers to any distraction from the reception and understanding of the message. The distraction may be some activity or condition in the receiver's environment, or it may be some condition internal to the receiver that affects reception and understanding.

Music blaring, children playing, telephone ringing, interruptions by other people, conversations between nearby people and other promotional messages are examples of outside noise. Noise can also result from some condition associated within the receiver. Illness, anger, worry, preoccupation, discomfort, or uneasiness, for example, will tend to affect the way the message is received. Any distracting influence present as a message is being transmitted may distort the meaning of the message, lessen its impact, or actually prevent its reception.

Feedback

Feedback refers to the clues that indicate to the source whether or not the message is being received and the degree to which it is understood. Such clues may suggest changes in the presentation that will make the message more meaningful to the receiver and more consistent with the source's intent.

In-face-to-face situations the sequential steps in the process are simply repeated *with the original source* and receiver exchanging roles. The clue may be nothing more than a frown, a raised eyebrow, or a nod of the head; nevertheless, it is a message in every sense of the word. Or feedback may be orally expressed by the original receiver in the form of questions or statements. The good salesperson takes full advantage of the feedback and adjusts the presentation accordingly.

When it is necessary to use mass media, however, acquiring feedback is a problem. Yet it is essential that the source have some idea as to whether the target audience is getting the correct message. Since there is no direct contact between source and receiver, feedback must be obtained through indirect methods such as marketing research, opinion surveys, attitude studies, and perhaps sales of the product. Clearly, feedback obtained in this manner is much less reliable and timely than that received through direct contact.

Decoding

Decoding the reverse of encoding, takes place at the receiver's and of the channel. The source, who wants to implant an idea in the receiver's mind, puts the idea into message form, encodes the message, and transmits it. If all goes well, the source's idea will be reproduced in the receiver's mind and communication will have occurred.

If perfect communication is to take place, the message must be decoded in precisely the same way that it was encoded. Because no two people perceive things exactly the same way, the best thing that can be hoped for is that some degree of congruency will be achieved.

The decoding process begins as soon as the receiver becomes aware of the message. He or she "translates" the message, into an idea, and if the idea matches that which the source had in mind, communication has taken place.

The terms denotative and connotative are significant in both the encoding and decoding processes. The denotative meaning of a word is that which is universally accepted; it is the meaning that identifies the object to which the word refers. The connotative meaning of a word is its unique meaning to an individual, stemming from emotions of feelings rather than thought. For example, the denotative meaning of snow, is "precipitation in the form of white flakes which can accumulate on the ground to several inches or feet." The connotative meaning of snow, on the other hand, is not the same to all individuals. To home-owners it may suggest the unpleasant task of shoveling the sidewalks and driveway. But to the children in the home it may mean snowballs and sledding.

If the encoder uses the word snow in the message, there is no assurance whatsoever that the decoder will translate it exactly in the manner intended. Communication may not take place because the idea the source had might not be recreated in the mind of the receiver. The encoder must make every effort to use the language, signs, and symbols that not only have the correct denotative meaning, but also will likely have connotative meanings to the. receiver that are consistent with the idea the source is attempting to transmit.

Receiver

It is impossible to divorce the decoder from the receiver as people because the receiver is the decoder. However, it is possible to discuss them separately, it we consider decoding as an activity and the receiver as a person.

We have established that the message must be encoded in terms of the receiver. If this is done well, the receiver is in a likely position to decode the message as the source intended. "Encoding the message in terms of the receiver" means using language, signs and symbols whose denotative and connotative meanings are shared by both source and receiver-not meanings that are simply those of the source. The only way that communication will take place is for both source and receiver to use the same referents in the encoding the decoding processes. A referent is the particular object, event, or concept that signs and symbols identify or describe.

Suppose that a restaurant operator has decided to add a line Mexican dishes to the menu. One of the advertisements promoting the new line states. "Our chili is always hot." Such a statement seems simple enough. However, unless the audience had been identified very carefully, communication would not take place with all receives because the referents for the words chili and hot might not be the same for both source and receiver.

Chili is thought of by some people as a soup, to be consumed as such; to other people it describes a special kind of meat sauce to be put on tamales and other kinds of Mexican food. The word hot might refer to the temperature of the chili, or it might refer to the strength of the ingredients used in the product. Thus, there are at least four different messages that could be decoded from the one simple statement, depending on the referents used in the process.

The foregoing illustration suggest that a receiver may receive a message but not the message. If such is the case, of course, communication has not taken place because the idea in the source's mind has not been recreated in the mind of the receiver. Referents derive from the influence of one's culture and are tempered by a unique background and experience. This is why it is so difficult to communicate with people whose culture is different from ours. Languages is an obvious difference, but the differences need not be that extreme. The many subcultures in any society present problems of communication because of the different referents associated with the same signs and symbols. In mass communication the logical approach to the problem is market segmentation.

Perception

Communication is complete only if the receiver perceives the message as the source intended. Berelson and Steiner define perception as "The more complex process by which people select, organize, and interpret sensory stimulates into a meaningful and coherent picture of the world." It is generally agreed that perception begins upon detection of stimuli by the senses, but a person cannot possibly detect all of the stimuli to which he or she is exposed. Why, then, are people obvious to some stimuli and susceptible to others? Why do people "attend" some promotional messages and ignore others? The answer lies in the concept selective perception.

Selective perception

The observer, in the face of the countless stimuli to which exposure is possible, sorts out particular aspects of the environment to be perceived. Initially, of course, the individual even selects certain stimuli for physical exposure. Beyond that, selective perception is used in allowing some stimuli to which exposures was made to enter conscious awareness-choosing promotional messages to allow to "come through." How many of the five to eight television commercials given during a station break do you really perceive even though you are physically exposed to all of them? Selection is based on a number of factors, but significant among them are your physical and psychological needs and your attitudes.

In choosing the stimuli one wishes to enter conscious awareness, each person not only consider those that the he or she wants to see but also those not to see. A person seeks consistency in the things he or she knows, and if one is a aware of a number of things that are not psychologically consistent, frustration may arise. One way the person may attempt to relieve the discomfort is by revising the perception of relevant stimuli. The person may choose to distort perceived stimuli or simply to ignore them. For example, the confirmed cigarette smoker who is aware that he or she is more likely to contact lung cancer than the nonsmoker, but who does not want to quite smoking, experiences frustration. To reduce the discomfort, the smoker may seek out stimuli that can be perceived as supporting the habit, distort perception of the conflicting stimuli, or ignore the stimuli entirely.

The phenomenon is operative in many aspects of promotion. An aspirin buyer, for example, may perceive only "Bayer" as suitable and discard messages suggesting that other brands are equally effective. An avid member of a political party avoids exposure to the speeches of a candidate of the opposing party or perhaps distorts the message when exposure is unavoidable. And so on.

Attitudes

Perception is also affected by attitudes, those "enduring systems of positive or negative evaluations, emotional feelings, and poor contraction tendencies with respect to social objects." Having an attitude means that the individual is no longer neutral towards the object of the attitude but is either for it or against it. Furthermore, if the attitude is a strong one, the individual resists any attempts to change it; and this influences what is perceived and how.

Since an attitudes is a tendency to behave in a certain way under a given set of circumstance, it is important that the promotional strategist correctly determine consumer attitudes in order to design appropriate communication strategy. As Rom Markin says, "A large amount of communication must function either to reinforce existing attitudes and behavior or to accelerate or stimulate the behavior sequences of consumers who are already predisposed to act in a given manner"

Thus in order to be totally successful in any communication effort, the source must not only understand the communication process but must also have some knowledge of the many forces working on the receiver that have a bearing on the reception of the message.

Promotion is communication. If communication does not take place, the promotional effort will fail. This is true whether the object of the effort is a product, a service, or an idea-whether it is a can of green beans, a guided tour of the Orient, or a plea to support the United fund. Thus it is essential that the promotional strategist have some knowledge of the communication process.

The basic elements in all communication situations are sources, message, encoding, channels, decoding, receiver, noise, and feedback. The source is the originator of the message, which was defined as an idea in transmittable form. Encoding is the process of putting the message into a form that can be received and understood. The channel is the means by which the message is transmitted. Usually, in addition to the primary channel there are several secondary channels. Noise is any distraction that interests with the reception and understanding of the message; it may be in the external environment of the receiver or may result from some internal condition of the receiver. Feedback refers to the clues the source gets that indicate whether or not the message is being received. Decoding is the reverse of encoding and takes place are the receiver's end of the channel.

Perception is significant in communication for many reason, but it is particularly significant in explaining why an individual is aware of some messages and ignores others. The term selective perception describes this phenomenon. Among the many criteria in the selection process are attitudes. Having an attitudes means that the individual is not longer neutral with respect to the attitude object; and perception is influenced by a desire to maintain consistency.

7 Promotion Objectives

Most of us have objectives in life, and the more clearly defined our objectives are, the more directed our behaviour is. However, our objectives are often vague, and our behaviour is less effective with respect to accomplishing them than it would be if we were more precise in defining them. A college student, for example, whose professed objective is to "get through school" would exhibit much less disciplined behaviour toward that objective than would one who was striving to graduate with a 3.5 grade point average. The point is that the more carefully we define our objectives, the more likely it is that we will accomplish them because we can do a better job of directing all relevant aspects of our behaviour to that end.

Clearly defined objectives are especially important in organizations. Accomplishment is only possible if all subdivisions of the group or business establish their own objectives in relation to the overall objectives of the organization. If goals are stated in vague terms, the behaviour they precipitate can be muddled or counter productive.

Purposes of objectives

Among the many reasons for having objectives, three seem to be particularly significant to organizations: (1) they provide incentive for action; (2) they stimulate coordinated effort; and (3) they facilitate measurement of performance.

Provide incentive for action

Having an objective gives us direction as well as enthusiasm. Objectives are really results we expect to achieve. In fact, results may be considered to be synonymous with objectives but separated by time and cost.

Thus, if an objective established for a business is to realize a 15 percent return on investment during the next fiscal year, the expected result is that the firm well earn a 15 percent return. Furthermore, if that objective has been established and communicated to the appropriate personnel in such a way as to generate enthusiastic acceptance, it will provide incentive for action on the part of those individuals.

Stimulate coordinated effort

Since a business firm, or any other organization, is composed of people, there will necessarily be a number of individual goals represented in the organization. These personal goals will cause a certain amount of conflict of effort among individuals in the performance of their activities.

However, *successful* companies are able to identify objectives to which most individuals in the organization subscribe. There are two possible reasons for this ability:" (1) company goals reflect a consensus of individual goals, or (2) company goals reflect the goals of influential individuals who impose them on noninfluentials.

In either case, of course, the degree of coordination of effort depends upon the extent to which the objectives are accepted. Acceptance does not just happen. Proper leadership and rapport with subordinates are necessary to achieve coordination of effort toward a goal. In fact, it is the president's duty to first see that objectives are set and accepted and then to provide the necessary resources to reach them.

Facilitate measurement of performance

It is impossible to evaluate performance in the absence of objectives. If we do not know where we are supposed to be when we get there, how can we know how much farther we have to go? Thus, one of the major functions of objectives is to provide a benchmark against which we can judge the effectiveness of our actions. If we only realize a 10 percent return on our investment but our objective was a 15 percent return, we know our performance was not as good as expected. An analogous situation would be a student whose objective was to get an A in a curse but who only got a B. Without the objective, the performance might have been judged satisfactory.

Characteristics of good objectives

Objectives are no good unless they are soundly conceived. Indeed, poorly conceived objectives often have a more adverse effect on performance than no objectives at all, even to the point of being counterproductive.

Harmony of objectives

All business firms and other organizations have many objectives and many "layers" of objectives. At the top, for example, objectives might be established in terms of return on investment, share of market, or growth. In addition to these then, each functional area will have its objectives. If these functional areas are subdivided in any way, the subdivisions, likewise, will have objectives.

In view of such a multiplicity of objectives, it is essential that there be consistency among them. One way to maximize consistency is to establish subobjectives in such a way that their accomplishment will result in the accomplishment of the overall objectives." A basic condition associated with such a procedure is that the management in each area for which an objective is established must have command over the resources necessary to accomplish the objective.

Specific characteristics

In addition to the underlying requirement of consistency, there are certain specific characteristics that good objectives have.

Stated in concrete and measurable terms

Since one purpose of objectives is to facilitate measurement of performance, they must be started in such a way as to allow for meaningful measurement and evaluation. This means that such vague statements as "increase brand awareness" or "enlarge our market share" are unacceptable as objectives. Rather, they should be stated in more specific terms such as "to increase brand awareness by 20 percent among consumers 18 to 30 years of age in the Unites States during 198-," or "to increase market share by 10 percent in the first six months of 198-"

Fair and reasonable

Objectives should be set high enough to demand he best efforts of the individuals involved, but not so high as to result in discouragement. This characteristic is particularly significant when accomplishment of the objective is dependent upon the efforts of one individual, such as a salesperson. An objective impossible to accomplish does not stimulate incentive but kills it and concomitantly lowers morale. It is not easy to set ideal objectives in this regard.

Clearly stated in understandable

If a person is expected to work toward the accomplishment of an objective, certainly that individual should understand what is required.

Written

Too many firms fail to write their objectives. Word-of-mouth communication tends to distort the intended message. Moreover, people forgot. The only way to make certain that each person affected by the stated objective remembers it, ad remembers it correctly, is to see that each one has a copy of the objective in writing.

Objectives in the promotion mix

We have seen that promotion mix consists of advertising, personal selling, sales promotion, and publicity. Objectives should be established in each of these areas, and the objectives established for each element of the promotion mix should collectively reflect the objective established for the promotion function likewise, the objectives established for the promotion function should. In conjunction with those established for the other elements of the marketing mix reflect the objectives established for the marketing function, and so on.

Advertising objectives

Obviously, businesses advertise because management believes that advertising will ultimately increase sales . The belief is generally true. In the long run, effective advertising does act favourably on sales although it may be as Ross Garrell suggests, that the effect is to reduce sales cost. Nevertheless, an objective expressed in term of sales may not be logical for advertising.

Advertising versus marketing objectives

When sales objectives are established for advertising, they are usually, rather, marketing objectives. Despite the likely assumption that sales increases occur because of effective advertising, the increases can rarely be attributed solely to advertising. The marketing manager responsible for developing the strategy to produce an increase in sales uses every tool in the marketing mix. Such sales increases as may take place, therefore, may be due to a reduction in price, a change in channels of distribution, a change in the product, or a faster method of delivering the product-all in addition to, or instead of, advertising. Thus it would be difficult, if not impossible, to identify any one tool as the only factor producing the sales increase.

If one of the reasons for establishing objectives is to facilitate measurement of performance, how can the effectiveness of advertising be determined if its contribution to the sales increase cannot be isolated? If after an advertising campaign sales did in fact increase by 10 percent, how much of that increase was due to advertising alone? It is simply not possible to know.

Similar reasoning can be applied to the promotion of ideas-or to advertising for nonprofit organizations. Politicians have made extensive use of advertising in recent years in connection with their election campaigns. They advertise to increase the number of voters who support hem. But advertising is just one of the tools they use. They also use personal selling, sales promotion, and publicity. Thus, it is not possible to attribute a favourable vote on election day solely to advertising.

Communications objectives

Advertising objectives should relate to advertising's role in the marketing function. Each subdivision of marketing would be assigned a specific part to play in the total marketing program, and advertising's part should be that of communication. Thus, advertising objectives should be stated in communication terms and effectiveness measured in those terms so that it is separated from the other variables in the marketing mix.

Russell H. Colley, for example, in *defining advertising Goals for measured advertising results* suggest that not only should an advertising objective be a specific communications task but also that the audience in which it is to be accomplished should be delineated and that time limits be imposed for its accomplishment. This, the advertising objective might be to increase by 20 percent during the current campaign year the number of mothers with elementary school-age children in the Pacific Northwest who know that Brand x toothpaste contains fluoride.

Objectives and the long-term effects of advertising

The total effect of an advertising program is not always immediately noticeable. People are not generally persuaded to rush right out to buy a product. As a matter of fact, it may take several years for this to happen.

Lavidge and Steiner proposed a number of years ago that people go through a series of steps in arriving at the decision to buy and that advertising can be a force that moves them up these steps. Their model, reproduced in part as figure, that shows this movement together withe the appropriate types of advertising for each step.

The implication, of course, is that advertising objectives should be related to the steps. If people are unaware of the product, for example, the specific advertising objective should be to make people aware of the product, for example, the specific advertising objective should be to make people aware and not necessarily to sell. The objectives would change, then, as people in a market move up the steps. The final objective may be a sales objective-to "trigger" the sale-since at this point advertising may be somewhat isolated in the marketing mix.

Secondary objectives

It is quite likely than an advertising program will have several objectives, although it is equally likely that one will predominate. And accomplishment of the predominant objective usually provides direction for the advertising program with respect to the theme used, the media chosen, and other facets of the program. Thus, advertisers attempt to select the media that will result in the least amount of waste circulation with respect to accomplishing the major objective-that is, to minimize the number of nonprospects for the product whom the medium reaches.

In the final analysis, setting advertising objectives is simply crystallizing expectations into a form that can provide direction for effort and a benchmark for the measurement of effectiveness.

Personal selling objectives

Although advertising objectives usually should be communications objectives, the situation is different with respect to personal selling. The interview between salesperson and client is a face-to-face encounter, and the effectiveness of the promotional effort can be identified with sales much more easily than is true in the case of advertising. However, if a sale results from the interview, it is due largely to the persuasive communication of the salesperson. Thus sales, even when established as an objective, may simply be a measure of communication effectiveness.

The foregoing statement notwithstanding, and despite the fact that advertising may have played a part in the purchase decision of the customer, it is entirely logical to state personal selling objectives in terms of sales or sales-related activities.

Sales objectives can take several forms, including (1) sales volume in either dollars or units, (2) sales volume less direct expenses, and (3) contribution margin. Objectives stated in terms of sales related activities include number of calls made, number of new accounts, and other activities that are not necessarily actual selling.

Sales volume

The easiest objective to set for personal selling is sales volume; this is usually synonymous with quota. There is no inconsistency here because objectives are really results we expect to achieve. For example, objectives might be established for each salesperson, the total of which would be the objective for the firm. The process of setting the objectives is complicated. It involves a consideration of sales persons' territories, sales districts and regions, and many other things.

Sales volume less direct expenses

The purpose of establishing a sales objective that considers expenses is to strive for some degree of control over the expense salespeople incur in generating sales. Such expenses include travel, meals, lodging, and entertainment. To be sure, greater sales can often be achieved by spending more to get them, but at some point the increasing expenses would nullify and profit. Thus stating the quota in such a way as to recognize the impact of expenses on profit makes the salesperson aware of the need to be careful with expense money.

But there is a danger here. The salespeople must not be so conscious of the need to minimize expenses that they unwisely reduce spending. Certain expenses are necessary, and too much budget cutting could reduce sales volume.

Contribution margin

Contribution margin is equal to the salesperson's gross margin less the expenses over which the salesperson has control. Gross Margin is essentially the difference between the price the customer pays for the product and the company's cost to produce it. Thus, the difference between the gross margin of the product and the salesperson's expenses in the sales is the amount that is contributed to the recovery of the overall fixed costs of the firm.

Objectives, or quotas, stated in these terms tend to encourage the salesperson to push the high-margin items. Because the easiest items to sell often carry the lowest margin, objectives stated in terms of sales volume encourage salespeople to ignore those products that earn more money for the company. The emphasize profit instead of units sold, objectives are sometimes stated in terms of contribution margin.

Sales-related activities

Personal selling objectives are occasionally established for other activities required of salespeople in addition to making sales. An objective may be for example, for each salesperson in a particular territory to call on a specified number of accounts every day. The rationale for such an objective, of course, is that the more accounts contracted by the salesperson the more sales he or she will make. In addition, such an objective tends to discourage visiting too long with any one buyer.

It is possible that this kind of objective can have an adverse effect on sales, however. Some buyers enjoy talking with salespeople; and the salesperson's need to hurry through the interview in order to contact the required number of accounts may antagonize those buyers, possibly to the point that they cease to be customers.

Another sales-related objective is calling on a specified number of potential new customers in order to generate new business. Use of this objective depends on the circumstances in the sales territory. For example, if a salesperson is working in a territory in which a majority of the potential customers have already been "signed up," a new customer objective would serve no useful purpose.

Other sales-related activities that could be the basis for objectives include such things as increasing order size, increasing the number of service calls, reducing the quantity of merchandise returned, and reducing selling costs-all by specified percentages or amounts.

Sales promotion objectives

Sales promotion, the third element in the promotion mix, consists of "those marketing activities other than personal selling, advertising, and publicity that stimulate consumer purchasing and dealer effectiveness, such as displays, shows, exhibitions, demonstrations, and various nonrecurrent selling efforts not in the ordinary routine.

Sales promotion efforts are aimed at such diverse groups that it is difficult to generalize with respect to objectives. Targets include company employees, dealers, and consumers. The role of sales promotion is to provide a direct inducement for response from these targets.

Thus, unlike most advertising, most sales promotion efforts are planned to stimulate *immediate* action. The objective, therefore, can usually be expressed in terms of sales because if action does take place in connection with the sales promotion effort it is a measure of communication effectiveness. Although it is rarely possible to entirely isolate the effects of the use of one marketing tool from the others, the results of sales promotion activities are the easiest to separate.

When such "nonrecurrent" selling efforts as point-of-purchase materials, contests, premiums, and deals are used to stimulate purchase, the objectives established in connection with their use should be specific and measurable and usually stated in terms of sales.

Publicity objectives

Objectives for the remaining element in the promotion mix, publicity, should also be stated in communication terms. As a matter of fact it is difficult to set objectives logically for publicity since the promotion manager has little control over media use. Because the use of publicity requires the assent of one or more outsiders such as an editor or a reporter, the successful accomplishment of any objective set for publicity is contingent not only upon the reasonableness of the objective but also on the decision of media representatives to publish the material.

Nevertheless, objectives should be set if publicity is to be used. Moreover, since a direct relationship between the effects of publicity and sales is difficult to establish, the objectives should be stated in terms of communication, not sales. Publicity can be quite effective in making consumers aware of new products, changes in existing products, and company activities if these things are newsworthy; and a good promotion manager can often persuade the media decision-makers that they are.

The promotion objective

Although to discuss the promotion mix we must divide it into its elements, it is the combined effect of the results from each element of the promotion mix that causes the accomplishment of the objectives established for the promotion function. Obviously then, objectives should complement one another. Every effort should be made to make certain that the objectives established for any one element of the promotion mix are not only compatible with those set for the other elements but also complement them. Indeed, if the objectives are properly set, the effect will be synergistic-the result will be greater than the sum of the effects of accomplishing each objective individually.

As the maximum efficiency of a system depends upon the effective harmonizing of its parts, the system of marketing is most efficient if all of its parts have specific complementary roles. Each part of the system must carry out its role to reach the system's goal. As one part of marketing, promotion is given its role, and each part of promotion has a specific role and specific objective.

The task of marketing, in general, is find out what the consumer wants, develop an appropriate product or service, and see that it reaches as many consumers as possible. Marketing's job is a broad one, but when it is broken down into parts to be accomplished by the subdivisions of marketing the job does get done. Promotion's part in the overall task is communication-making the consumer aware of the existence of the product and informing the consumer of the reasons why it fits his or her needs. The four tools of promotion are utilized for this purpose, and each of them is given a specific part to play in the total process. Objectives are then established.

The only way any organization can accomplish its purposes is to establish objectives in order to direct behaviour. Sound objectives provide incentive for action, stimulate coordinated effort, and facilitate measurement of performance.

Objectives should be established for each element of the promotion mix. Advertising objectives should be stated in communications terms since it is difficult to measure the direct effect of advertising upon sales. There are too many variables associated with generating sales; and when a sales objective is stated for advertising it is usually a misplaced marketing objective.

Personal selling objectives are usually stated in terms of sales or sales-related activities because any sales resulting from the use of this tool can be attributed more directly to the salesperson than to other promotion activities.

Sales promotion objectives are usually sales objectives since (1) immediate sales are normally the desired result and (2) sales provide a measure of the communication effectiveness of the devices.

Publicity is difficult to control, but objectives should be established nevertheless. Since it is difficult to relate sales to publicity efforts, the objectives should be communications objectives, dealing with making consumers aware of the existence of new products, changes in existing products, and newsworthy activities.

The objectives established for each element of the promotion mix should collectively reflect the objectives established for the promotion function.

8 Promotion and Marketing

The purpose of promotion is to persuade, promotion means communication about products, services, and ideas. Naturally promotion involves many creative aspects, such as copywriting and layout in advertising and the development of sales presentations in personal selling. Although these areas are extremely important, this book will focus on promotion as a function.

Persuasion

Promotion persuades. It also provides information, but its emphasis must be on persuasion. As we shall see later, the kind of information presented is determined by its persuasive potential in a given situation.

Persuasion is the ultimate objective of promotion whether we are dealing with products, or services, or ideas. In each case we are attempting to persuade people to accept our intended message and to respond, or react, accordingly. We want to convince them that out product or service can do a better job of satisfying their wants than can the alternatives. We want them to believe that the ideas we are presenting-social, religious, political, or whatever-are worthy and desirable.

But to say the purpose of promotion is to persuade is not to endorse unethical practices to assure success. Not only are such practices morally wrong, they are not good strategy.

Promotion and the consumer

Exposure to promotional messages is inescapable in today's society. We are the targets of messages from dawn to dusk. We turn on the radio in the morning to get the news and hear several commercials. Scanning the newspaper before going to work or class, we see advertisements. On the way we pass by a billboard to two and some shop signs. Throughout the day we use ball point pens, calendars, or magazines-all of which may have advertising messages. In the evening, we put up with countless commercials in order to watch our favorite television programs. In addition to this bombardment, it is quite likely that we will enter a store, see innumerable sales messages on signs and packages, and be approached by a salesperson who will attempt to persuade us to buy.

So we all know what promotion is. But do we? We really see only the end product of a complicated activity. It is somewhat like a spectator sport; as we watch the game, we really have on appreciation for each team's hard work and preparation. We take if for granted that the players are ready, and we subconsciously assume that their playing skills just happen.

Because promotion is tooted in the marketing function, to understand promotion it is necessary to understand its relationship to marketing.

The marketing function

Effective management of any activity requires a proper perspective of the system in which it operates. We must understand the marketing system before examining promotion's role in the total program.

A systems perspective

The essence of systems analysis is that the whole is composed of a number of parts and that each part must work with the others for the system to work. Thus, maximum effectiveness requires perfect coordination of all the parts-an impossible achievement in the behavioral sciences, of course, but something to be strived for, nevertheless.

We could consider the whole of society as a system whose component parts include government, education, religion, and business. Each of these parts would be composed of separate parts and would constitute a system itself-a subsystem of the system of society. The concept could be continued through each successive layer of activity. Marketing would be included in the parts that make up the subsystem of business, and it must be harmonized with business's other components so that business can operate effectively.

Marketing as a system

There are as many definitions of marketing as

there are writers of marketing textbooks; indeed, there are more definitions than there are marketing textbooks. They all have the common meaning, however, that marketing is the system by means of which products, services, or ideas are conceived, publicized, moved, distributed, and transmitted to appropriate market segments. Thus marketing is a system necessarily composed of a number of subsystems, each of which must harmonize with the others for maximum effectiveness of the system.

Marketing begins before the product is developed, the service designed, or the idea formalized. It continues until consumer satisfaction is assured. Marketing begins and ends with the consumer; to consider it in any other light is to court failure in the system. Students of marketing will recall that the concept of market segmentation is consumer-oriented and is based on the notion that a group of people with similar motives for purchasing a product or service or accepting a particular idea make up a market segment. The market may include the entire population or it may consist of a very few people. The important point is that the criteria for segmentation relate to reasons for purchasing a product or accepting an idea.

A model of the marketing system

Let us now see exactly how promotion fits into the marketing system and how it relates to the other components.

Marketing both acts and is act upon, since the very notion of a system implies a creative force and an arena in which it operates. To get the total picture of the marketing system, therefore, it is not only necessary to identify the components of the system, but also to delineate the arena. The operation of the marketing system in its environment is illustrated in the analogy shown in the following figure. The figure portrays, among other things, the need for all components of the system to work together.

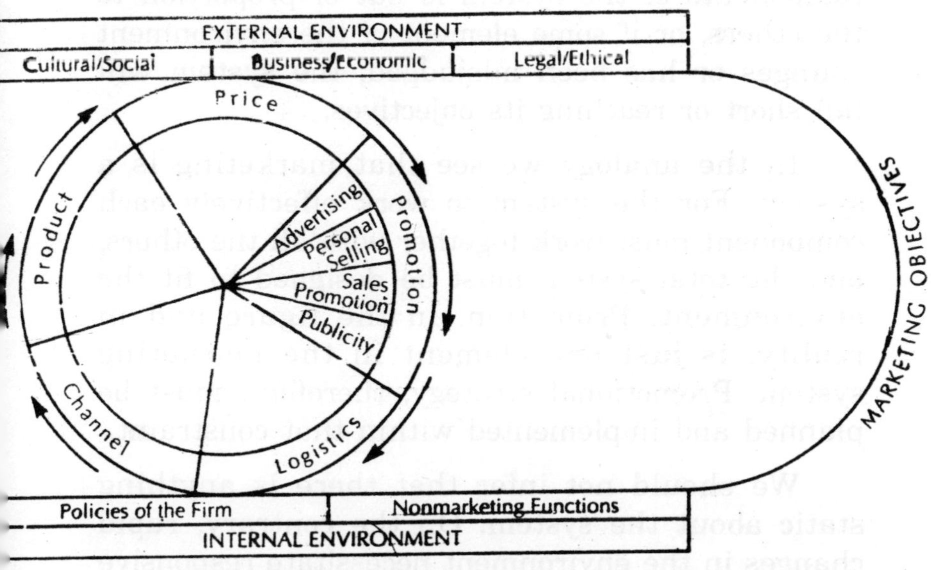

An analogy of the marketing system

As you examine the figure, visualize a wheel moving between two grooved tracks toward a receptacle designed to receive it at the end of the tracks. If the wheel is properly designed, it will roll into the receptacle. On the other hand, if one of the spokes is out of line, or if the condition of the tracks changes, the wheel will become lodged in the tracks and its movement toward the receptacle will cease.

The wheel represents the marketing system; the tracks symbolize the environment in which the system operates; and the receptacle denotes the marketing objectives. If the marketing system is properly conceived, with due consideration given to its environment, the marketing objectives will be accomplished. On the other hand, if one of the components of the system is out of proportion to the others, or if some element of the environment changes or has been misjudged, the system will fall short or reaching its objectives.

In the analogy we see that marketing is a system. For the system to work effectively each component must work together with all the others, and the total system must be designed to fit the environment. Promotion, in the figure and in reality, is just one element in the marketing system. Promotional strategy, therefore, must be planned and implemented within that constraint.

We should not infer that there is anything static about the system. On the contrary, rapid changes in the environment necessitate responsive changes in the system and require constant monitoring. The task of marketing management is to plan and effect the appropriate changes.

So the two groups of factors significant to the marketing function are those delineating the environment and those comprised by the marketing system. Let us examine these factors in somewhat more detail in order to understand more fully promotion's part in the scheme of things.

Environmental factors

Environmental factors exert enormous influence on the operation of the marketing system, yet they cannot be manipulated. They are the forces that act upon the system. Those individuals responsible for managing the marketing function must have a thorough knowledge of the environment's actual and potential impact and make decisions accordingly. These managers cannot change the environment, but they must know that it will change. The two group of environmental factors are those that exist outside the organization and those that operate within it.

External factors

External factors can be classified very broadly into three categories; cultural/social, business/economic, and legal/ethical.

Cultural / Social: Culture refers to the composite ways of living as they have been determined by a group of human beings over the years and transmitted from one generation to another,. Attributes of culture are not innate, but are learned from parents and from other people and are passed on to offspring and to other people.

Because of the interrelationships that necessarily exist among people, culture is highly social. The people in any group associated with a particular "culture" have adopted, deliberately or undesignedly, the attributes of the culture. Such adoption of cultural dictates stems from many causes, one of which is the desire for peer group acceptance or other group relationship.

Business/economic: The activities of other businesses, both individually and collectively, must be considered beyond the control of marketing management. They are a part of the environment, however and are reflected in the many facets of competition with which the firm must deal. The number and kinds of retailers, wholesalers, and other business institutions, for example, may be virtually fixed, and the firm attempting to perform in that arena must accept it as it is and plan a marketing strategy accordingly

Economic aspects must be considered in connection with marketing decision making. It is, after all, the willingness of people to buy makes a marketing effort successful; and willingness to buy is affected by economic factors. Such general conditions as prosperity, recession, and depression, for example, are extremely significant in this regard. Tax and spending policies of the federal government, inflation, the availability of money, agricultural crop conditions, recurring shortages of essential materials, and many other economic forces affect demand. All are beyond the control of marketing management; yet they must be considered as marketing decisions are made.

Legal/Ethical: The third broad category of factors characterizing the external environment is identified as legal/ethical. These two terms are not synonymous. Some actions that are legal are not ethical, and vice versa. There is a relationship between the two concepts, however, since many actions viewed as unethical have been made illegal.

Promotion decisions and other marketing decisions must not only be made in string compliance with the law, but they must also be consistent with good business ethics. Failure in this regard encourages severe antibusiness criticism and, of course, possible . In recent years, the legal ethical environment of marketing has been increasingly significant. Consumer groups have influenced the passage of much legislation designed to regulate marketing activity, and industry itself has encouraged greater use of self-regulation to reduce the adverse criticism directed at marketing.

Internal factors

In addition to these external forces, there are conditions within firm itself that must be considered as part of the environment in which the marketing system operates. These conditions relate to those internal factors not directly related to the performance of the marketing relate to those internal factors not directly related to the performance of the marketing function and over which the marketing manager has no control. Such factors may be controllable, of course, and may be changed as the need arises-but not by authority of the marketing manager. They include the general company policies and those nonmarketing activities that affect and are affected by marketing decisions.

Company policies: Each company establishes policies to guide action in all the functional areas of the business, and marketing decisions must be consistent with these policies. General policies that place constraints on marketing decisions include those associated with growth, market share, extension of credit and credit terms, product, price, and relation with the various publics.

Nonmarketing functions: Further restrictions are placed on the freedom of the marketing manager in his or her decision making by the operation of other functional areas of the firm. In some instances these nonmarketing functional areas directly constrain marketing action, in others, marketing action is restricted because of its effect on the other functions.

Financial managers, for example, may severely limit the promotional budget. Marketing action in the area of promotion would thus be limited by the size of the budget they determine. On the other hand, although it does not directly constrain marketing action, a given production capacity should considered in developing marketing strategy

Components of the marketing system

Because promotion is a part of marketing, it is necessary to have some knowledge of the other elements in the marketing system to understand the role of promotion.

Marketing objectives

Essential in the development and constant

adjustment of the marketing system in its environment is a consideration of the marketing objectives.. When the objectives are changed, the marketing mix requires readjustment just as it does when conditions in the environment change. In fact, many changes in objectives are suggested by changes in the environment.

It is not our purpose here to discuss at length the process of setting marketing objectives. However, the objectives set for each of the subsystems of marketing should be consistent with the marketing mix should support the marketing objectives so that accomplishment by the subsystems contributes to the accomplishment of the marketing objectives.

Marketing mix

The factors making up the marketing system are refereed to as the marketing mix. Unlike the environmental factors that are beyond the control of the marketing manager, the elements of the marketing mix are the tools of marketing. It is through their manipulation that the system is kept on track. The task of marketing management is to maintain these elements in the proportion necessary for maximum effectiveness of the system. The problem is compounded, of course, by the constant changes taking place in the environment. As a change in the environment is perceived, the marketing manager rearranges the elements in the marketing system to counteract the change. Let us see how this might work.

We shall assume that sales are down in a

particular market segment. Something in the external environment has changed, and we must adjust our marketing mix to combat the change. We examine each element of the marketing mix.

Product: It could be that out product needs attention. Perhaps a competitor has entered our marketing with an improved product or one that is perceived as better than ours. We might make some improvements in our product, change the package or the size, or make some other change associated with the product itself that would revive its acceptance in the market segment.

Price: If it is the price of the competitor's product that has caused our sales to decline, we might adjust our price. This adjustment would probably be downward. However, raising the price might be effective if prestige is a reason for purchasing our product or if a price/quality association exists in connection with the product.

Channel: The problem might be that the channel of distribution-the number and kinds of firms through which our product passes to get to the consumer-are III-chosen. We nay be trying to sell our product through retail outlets that are not the kind consumers now use when buying such a product. For example we might package a line of small inexpensive toys in plastic bags and place them in toy stores and in the toy departments of department stores. If we later discovered that consumers seemed more likely to purchase our product priced and packaged as it is, in supermarkets than in toy stores, we would change the channel of distribution.

Logistics: The term logistics is used in marketing to refer to those activities associated with the physical movement of goods. Among the activities are transportation and warehousing. If our sales problem has been caused by poor logistics management, we might improve the situation by using a more rapid means of transportation than we have been using and at the same time reduce our warehousing costs.

Promotion: Finally, our hypothetical problem could be caused by a misuse of promotion. It could be that the situation calls for increased advertising expenditures. On the other hand, if the amount of money is adequate but it is not being spent for maximum effect, a change in the media carrying the advertising may be called for. Reducing the amount spent on advertising and increasing the number of sales-people in the territory might solves the problem. These are just a few of the changes that might be made if promotion is the culprit.

The elements as a system

Although each component in the marketing system is a subsystem with its own objectives and commensurate strategy, its actions must complement those of the other subsystems. If any of the actions it takes conflict with those of any of the other subsystem, the effectiveness of the total marketing system is reduced. A decision should not be made in one subsystem without first considering its effect on the operation of the others.

An obvious example will illustrate the point although it is the less obvious inconsistencies that are difficult to resolve. Suppose that after a thorough market analysis it was determined that a superior-quality product was necessary to obtain a share of a particular market segment, and thus product and all of its ramifications as an element of the marketing mix had been designed to create a certain image. Suppose that the promotion emphasized low, discount prices. Clearly the two subsystems would work against each other, and the result would be a less effective or ineffective marketing system.

Good marketing managers can increase the marketing system's effectiveness by using each of the subsystems in the way that can best accomplish the marketing objectives. Generally, this means making each of the subsystems responsible for a specific part of the overall task. If each of the subsystems performs effectively, then the total task will be accomplished. Promotion's part in the overall task is communication.

The promotion function

Knowledge about products, services, and ideas does not spontaneously reach those for whom it is intended. No matter how good the product, how valuable the service, or how sensible the idea, its creation or existence will remain unknown without deliberate effort to make the information available. Contrary to the old adage, the world no longer beats a path to the door of the better mousetrap builder unless the builder persuades the world that the mousetrap is better. It is the job of promotion to so persuade the world.

Promotion is the deliberate attempt on the part of an individual, business, or other institution to communicate appropriate information in a manner persuasive enough to induce the kind of acceptance, reaction, or response desired. Thus promotion is communication-persuasive communication-and its effectiveness depends upon the talent and skill of those who design it.

Components of the promotion system

Promotion is itself, a system whose components consist of advertising personal selling, sales promotion, and publicity.

Perhaps the most conspicuous of the components is advertising, which generally involves the use of mass media. The advertiser is always identified and pays for the opportunity of communicating a message.

Many firms rely heavily on advertising in their promotional, devoting a major portion of their promotion budget to its use. Such media as television, radio, newspapers, and magazines, for example, are used extensively by manufacturers of consumer goods. Numerous other media play significant roles in effective advertising programs.

Unlike advertising which is nonpersonal in nature, personal selling involves voice-to-voice contact. It may be a one-to-one situation, or it may be one individual attempting to persuade a group.

Furthermore, it may be a face-to-face contact or it may be done over the telephone.

Manufacturers of industrial goods are among those companies that use personal selling more than advertising in their promotional strategies.

Sales promotion consists of those promotional activities that are not considered advertising or personal selling. Such activities as games, contests, demonstrations, trade shows, trading stamps, and similar efforts are designed to help in promotional strategy.

Sales promotion is not to be confused with promotion-a broader term-of which sales promotion is a part.

Publicity resembles advertising in that it generally uses mass media and it is nonpersonal. It differs from advertising, however, in that it is not paid for by its sponsor. Publicity involves the favorable presentation in a print or broadcast medium of some newsworthy event associated with the business or institution.

Publicity is an effective tool because the favorable light in which the firm is thus shown is not seemingly created by the firm itself. However, it is difficult to use because it always involves a decision by one or more outside parties such as an editor.

The four components of the promotion system-advertising, personal selling, sales promotion, and publicity-are the tools of the promotion manager. Used in combination, they are referred to as the promotion mix. Like the marketing mix, the promotion mix must reflect a proper ration of the components.

There is no best component; nor is there any generally accepted best combination of components. Rarely is one tool used without the others. The timing of a consumer's decision to accept, react to or respond to the information is unpredictable-even by the expert who designs the promotion strategy. In addition, the degree of persuasiveness of the message varies with different tools used among different people at different times. Effective promotional strategy, therefore, generally requires the use of all the components. Each situation suggests its own proper mix.

Expanded concept of marketing

Most of us tend to associate marketing and all of its components with business firms. It has recently been suggested that the concept of marketing can be applied appropriately to many nonbusiness activities whose success depends upon the use of marketing-related approaches. Political candidates are promoted; church attendance is solicited; United Way campaigns are conducted; and response to many other civic and social causes is urged.

Therefore, although this book focuses on promotional strategy in business, the approaches, considerations, and techniques used in developing promotional strategy for business firms can be adapted and applied to the promotion of non-business causes and ideas.

Promotion is a part of marketing, and its strategy must be consistent with and complementary to marketing strategy. Providing information is a necessary part of the process, but the primary purpose of promotion is to persuade.

The marketing function is a system operating in an environment beyond the control of marketing. External factors in the environment are cultural/social, business/economic. And legal/ethical. Environmental factors within the firm itself that bear on marketing strategy include the general policies of the firm and certain nonmarketing functions.

The components of the marketing system include product, price, channel, logistics and promotion. These elements, referred to as the marketing mix, are the tools of marketing management. Promotion is one of the tools and must be used in conjunction with all the others.

Promotion is a system in itself. Its role in the overall marketing strategy is to communicate information in a persuasive manner. The components of the system include advertising, personal selling, sales promotion, and publicity. These elements, when combined into a promotional strategy, are referred to as the promotional mix and are the tools of promotion.

Finally, the concept of marketing may be expanded to include certain nonbusiness activities so that the techniques of promotional strategy may be applied to nonbusiness ventures that require persuading the public.

9 International Channels of Distribution

As for domestic marketing, the distribution process for international programs involves all those activities related to time, place, and ownership utilities for industrial and ultimate consumers. The selection, operation, and motivation of effective channels of distribution are often crucial factors in a firm's differential advantage in international markets. The diverse activities and culturally differentiated roles of channel intermediaries make the formulation of distribution strategies a challenge for any firm entering foreign markets.

The channels of distribution available in a country are the result of culture and tradition. For example, in Japan there are usually too many channels involved in the distribution of a product. In the developing countries, channels of distribution are scattered, small in scope, inefficient, and insufficient. An international distribution system must be adapted to the country's established practices. Channel innovations ought to emerge from customer need rather than through an arbitrary attempt to streamline the distribution system.

This chapter describes the alternative channels of distribution for an international marketer to consider. There are examples of different types of intermediaries, both domestic and foreign, for distribution across national boundaries. Guidelines are provided for selecting, motivating, and controlling the channels most appropriate for a firm's distribution mix. In addition, wholesale and retail patterns in overseas markets are examined. Also explored is the rationale of overseas franchising relationships along with their patterns of development. Finally the perspectives of international physical distribution are discussed. International distribution, which requires special knowledge of complex rate structures and tariffs, presents many unique problems. These call for an adequate management information system. Throughout the chapter, examples are given to illustrate how to achieve an effective distribution system in international markets.

Alternative distribution channels

Distribution channels are the link between producers and customers. There are various ways of creating this link. Basically, an international marketer distributes either directly or indirectly. Direct distribution amounts to dealing with a foreign firm. The indirect method means dealing through another U.S. Firm that serves as an intermediary. The choice of a particular channel link will be found upon considerations to be discussed in a later section of this chapter.

Channel theory

It has long been held that the channels of distribution available in a country depend on its stage of economic development, which is reflected in the per capita real income and the sociopsychological, cultural, or anthropological environment. From this premise, it can be concluded that:

- The more developed countries have more levels of distribution, more specialty stores and supermarkets, more department stores and more store in the rural areas.
- The influence of the foreign import agent declines with economic development.
- Manufacturer-wholesaler-retailer functions become separated with economic development.
- Wholesaler functions approximate those in North America with increasing economic development.
- Financing function of wholesalers declines and the size of the average store increases with increasing development.
- The number of small stores declines and the size of the average store increases with increasing development.
- The role of the peddler and Itinerant trader and the importance of the open-garden-fair decline with increasing development.

- Retail margins improve with increasing economic development.

According to this theory, changes in the channel structure of a country can be introduced only in response to changes in its economic and other environments. Channel changes cannot be enforced from without. At the cost of oversimplification, for example, supermarket distribution would not work in poor countries such as Egypt, Kenya, Sudan, and Pakistan because the economy and other environments operating in those countries are not conducive to such a form of distribution.

It is difficult for a supermarket fully to utilize its cost saving potential in a situation where the supply system for produce and meats is highly fragmented, agricultural products are badly graded, supermarkets are not part of a vertically integrated system and in many cases must compete with the small store owners for supplies in the central wholesale market. In addition, the supermarket must often bear high overhead costs, suffer from antiquated municipal laws limiting hours and modes of operations, face major employee training and motivation problems and must pay disproportionately higher taxes than the small food.

An empirical study on the subject, however, easts doubts on the viability of this theory. The results of the study showed little evidence to support the idea that the development of a marketing system in a country is determined by the limits of its social, economic, technological, and cultural environments. For example, it was found that channel structure and relationships mainly depend on the relative size of the firms at different channel stages, rather than on the country's level of development.

Despite the comprehensiveness and scope of the survey there was little evidence to support the widely held theory that the development of marketing structure closely parallels that of the social, economic, and cultural environment. Except in certain respects in Japan and Ceylon, the level of development of the marketing environment did not appear to be an important determinant of the organization of attitudinal characteristics of firms, or of channel; structure and relationships. Non were marketing structures of countries similar at comparable levels of development. In general, there was often a high degree of variation among firms within a country with regard to both firm characteristics and channel relationships.

These results suggest that the influence of environmental factors on marketing structure may be considerably less important than is frequently postulated. In particular, the variation among firms within a country suggests that individual firms may respond in different ways and in varying degrees to environmental conditions. No consistent pattern of response emerged at the national level.

Alternatively, the relationship between environmental factors and the marketing system may be more complex and indirect than that tested. The timing of technological conditions may be crucial factor. For example, the introduction of advanced marketing technology from a highly industrialized nation to a developing country may distort the relationship between the level of development and marketing structure. The appropriate methodology would be a study of the evolution of marketing structures over time in various countries rather than a comparative survey of countries at different levels of development.

Apparently, the relationship between a country's channel structure and its environment remains undefined. How else to explain the channels of distribution in a country is a matter of speculation. All that can be said, given the current state-of-the-art, is that distribution channels, like any other socioeconomic phenomenon, evolve slowly from a multitude of factors, some direct and some indirect. We do not quite know what these factors are, let alone their relationships.

Distribution channels in Japan: An example

Each country, rich or poor has its own unique distribution system, evolved over time. International marketers must carefully examine the various aspects of a country's established distribution system to determine how to obtain distribution for their goods.

Despite the fact that Japan is the second economic power in the world today, its distribution system, has been labeled outmoded, complex, cumbersome, and inefficient. The purpose of focusing this discussion on Japan is to emphasize that distribution structure is country-specific, and it would be native for international marketers to enforce their own new distribution system on a country. Thus, distribution channels must be used as they are and efforts should be made to fit into the country through the established patterns.

In general, the Japanese system encompasses a wide range of wholesalers and other agents, brokers, and retailers differing more in number than in function from their American counterparts. There are myriad tiny retail shops. An even greater number of wholesalers supplies goods to them, layered tier upon tier many more than most U.S. executives would think necessary. For example, soap may move through three wholesalers plus a sales company after it leaves the manufacturer before it even reaches the retail outlet. A steak goes from rancher to consumer in a process that often involves a dozen middle agents.

The Japanese distribution system stems from the early seventeenth century when cottage industries and a burgeoning urban population spawned a merchant class. And despite Japan's economic achievements, the distribution system has remained remarkably faithful to its antique pattern. The system endures in part because most Japanese companies typically operate with little equity capital and much debt. Manufacturers supply goods to wholesalers in return for promissory notes ranging up to about six months, thus, while wholesalers can mange on a relatively small amount of capital, manufacturers can spread their risks by dealing with many wholesalers. In this way, the financial structure complements the distribution system.

The distribution network also reflects other traditionally close ties among many Japanese companies. These ties go far beyond personal relationships. For example, Japanese wholesalers are usually willing to take back unsold goods from retailers the large number of wholesalers enables them to spread this risk, too. In addition, wholesalers often provide special rebates to retailers according to the stores sales volume and many small steelmakers get special financing from their own wholesalers when they expand production capacity.

The Japanese place much greater emphasis on the development of strong personal relationships with users in order to ensure a stable supply over a long period at a stable price. Their system fosters such relationships. Business in the United States tend to rely on price competitiveness and product satisfaction to establish supply.

The Japanese distribution system is built into the fabric of its society. It is a sort of welfare system that provides a living for so many people that the government does not have to pay welfare. In this way, the seemingly inefficient distribution system serves an important social function. It has been a flexible make-work device, acting as a buffer to absorb excess workers, particularly those on the verge of retirement. Many observes expect this social role to increase as the current slowdown in japan's economic growth shrinks employment in manufacturing.

Another reason for the longevity of Japan's distribution system is that it serves most companies well. Some suppliers, for instance, keep their inventories at or near their customers headquarters to ensure rapid deliveries. Foreigner companies of course, can't compete with such service unless they maintain substantial stockpiles and facilities in Japan.

Consumers also are served well. Lacking much storage space in their small homes, most Japanese homemakers shop several times a week and prefer convenient neighborhood shops. The little shops often strengthen their position by doing more for customers than just selling goods. In brief, Japanese distribution channels are more complex than comparable channels in the United States. But the dominant view in Japan is that the system suits the needs of Japanese consumers. For example while furniture stores in the United States may take up to ten weeks for delivery. Japanese consumers usually receive delivery within a week.

Moreover, statistics indicate that the distribution system is not likely to change soon. According to government figures, the number of mom-and-pop retailers employing four or fewer workers increased almost 50 percent between 1975 and 1985 to 2 million outlets. During the same period, the number of similar-size wholesalers rose to more than 200,000 from about 150,000. In 1984, the latest year for which complete figures are available, 5.1 million workers were employed in various wholesale operations and 7.5 million worked in retail outlets. The papa-mama stores control 56 percent of Japan's retail sales.

The way the Japanese distribution channels are structures and managed presents one of the major reasons for the failure of foreign firms to establish major market position in Japan.

Despite the fact that the Japanese channels have been held inefficient and cumbersome, they seem to serve the customer well. As the following illustration shows the Japanese concept of customer service supersedes any retail outlet in the United States.

My husband and I bought one souvenir the last time we were in Tokyo-a Sony compact disk player. The transaction took seven minutes at the Odakya Department Store, including time to find the right department and to wait while the salesman filled out a second charge slip after misspelling my husband's name on the first.

My in-laws, who were our hosts in the outlying city of Sagamthara mere eager to see their son's purchase, so he opened the box for them the next morning. But when he tried to demonstrate the player, it wouldn't work. We peered inside it had no innards. My husband used the time until the Odakya would open of 10.00 to practice for the rare opportunity in that country to was indignant. But at a minute to 10.00 he was prompted by the store ringing us.

My mother-in-law took the call and had to hold the receiver away from her ear against the barrage of Japanese honorific. Odakya's vice president was on his way over with a new disk player.

A taxi pulled up 50 minutes later and spilled out the vice president and a junior employee who was laden with packages and a clipboard. In the entrance hall the two men bowed vigorously.

The younger man was still bobbing as he read from a log that recorded the progress of their efforts to rectify their mistake, beginning at 4.32 P.M. the day before, when the salesclerk alerted the store's security guards to stop my husband at the door. When that didn't work, the clerk turned to his supervisor, who turned to his supervisor, until a SWAT team leading all the way to the vice president was in place to work on the only clues, a name and an American express card number. Remembering that the customer had asked him about using the disk player in the U.S. the clerk called 32 hotels in and around Tokyo to ask if a Mr. Kitasei was registered. When that turned up nothing, the Odakya commandeered a staff member to stay until 9 P.M. to call American Express headquarters in New York. American Express gave him our New York telephone number. It was after II when he reached my parents, who were staying at our apartment. My mother gave him my in-laws telephone number.

The younger man looked up from his clipboard and gave us, in addition to the new $280 disk player, a set of towels, a box of cakes, and a Chopin disk. Three minutes after this exhausted pair had arrived they were climbing back into the waiting cab. The vice president suddenly dashed back. he had forgotten to apologize for my husband having to wait while the salesman had rewritten the charge slip, but he hoped we understood that it had been the young man's first day.

My Tokyo experience contracts sharply with treatment I've received at home. In late July, without explanation or apology from Bloomingdale's a credit of $546.66 appeared on my American Express statement for china ordered January 12, paid for April 17, and never received.

Although no crucial differences in the functions of distribution exist among the European nations, the United States, and Japan, nevertheless distribution is directly connected with the final consumer and is naturally affected by social, cultural, and historical conditions peculiar to each country. The customs and practices in the distribution of products can differ substantially from one country to another, yet basically fulfill the same functions of channeling products from manufactures to consumers.

International channel members

The previous section mentioned two forms of distribution direct and indirect. Either way, a company may go through one or more agents or merchant intermediaries. The essential difference between them concerns the legal ownership of goods. In one method, an agent, without taking title to the goods, distributes them on behalf of the principal the manufacturer. In the other method, merchant intermediaries do business in their own names and hold title to the goods they deal in, identifies important types of intermediaries. The type of intermediaries and their names vary from country to country and from industry to industry in the same country. For this reason, the discussion here is limited to certain intermediaries popularly used worldwide for distribution across industries.

Indirect distribution through agents

Important among these types of agents are export management companies, manufacturers export agents, cooperative exporters. Webb-Pomerene associations, foreign freight forwarders, commission agents, and country-controlled buying agents and trading companies. While these agents do not take title, they do take possession of goods. However, they have different duties in respect to continuation of relationship with the principal, degree of control maintained by the principal , pricing authority accorded to the agent, affiliation with buyer or seller, number of principals served at a time, involvement or noninvolvement with shipping or handling of competitive lines; provision of promotional support; extension of credit to principal; and provision of market information.

Export management company. An export management company is an independent export organization that serves different companies in their export endeavors. The EMC regards the exporter as a client, not as an employer. The EMC deals in a number of allied but noncompetitive lines. Usually, the EMC handles the entire export function for a manufacturer. In all contracts and communications overseas, the EMC operates under the client's name, using client stationery and promotional materials, such as catalogs. EMCs differ in the scale of their operations. Some handle export sales for as few as four or five manufacturers, other serve as many as fifty companies. A typical from represents ten manufacturers. EMCs are especially helpful to small companies that are unable to afford experienced and skilled export managers. EMCs understand foreign cultures. They are up-to-date on international politics, logistics, taxation, and legal problems. They provide a viable alternative for small firms to launch themselves in the export business.

EMCs come in all sizes. The EMC provides a full range of services to manufacturers, relieving them of all the tasks involved in the process. The EMC obtains orders for their principals/clients by making contacts overseas and fills the orders, observing necessary formalities in packaging, documentation, and shipping.

An EMC may be just a one-person operation, or it may employ as many as a hundred people. Some firms are relatively new, while others have decades of experience. Large export management firms often maintain overseas officers in strategic locations. Senior executives of these firms frequently travel overseas to seek orders and develop relationships with the customers.

There are about 1,200 EMCs in the United States. Most are located in the larger seaport cities. The important sources for locating an EMC are the U.S Department of commerce, port authorities, and banks handling foreign trade. The national federation of export management companies, based in Washington. D.C. and local chambers of commerces are also good sources. An exporter should attempt to find an EMC that specializes in its product type, has in place a well-organized and controlled worldwide distribution system, is well-financed and managed, and is willing and eager to devote significant amounts of managerial effort and money to launching its product.

EMCs generate their income either from commissions or from discounts on goods they buy for resale overseas. The commission/discount varies from 10 percent or less to 30 percent or more, based on the service provided and the difficulty of the marketing task.

Benefits of export management companies

- *Credit assistance.* The EMC often does its own financing. It pays the manufacturer in dollars before the export order leaves the United States, relieving the client of any credit risk. Depending on the specific product category, the foreign buyer may need as much as 180 days' credit, or more. By providing the credit, the EMC helps bring buyer and seller together.

- *Licensing:* Import barriers, transportation charges, or local competition may make the effective promotion and sale of the manufacturer's goods impractical or impossible. The EMC will, when warranted by the sales potential of the market, frequently arrange for the loyal production of the manufacture's products under either a joint venture or a royalty-yielding license arrangement with the U.S. manufacturer. Armed with knowledge of the market through continuing activities in it, the EMC normally supervisors the implementation of such contracts and monitors performance on behalf of the U.S. manufacturer.

- *Demonstrations:* Some EMCs also arrange for overseas demonstrations and proper technical indoctrination of foreigner users or representatives, by either the *EMC*'s or the manufacturer's technical staff, depending on the nature of the products.

- *Shipping expenses*: The EMC saves its clients money by consolidating shipments. It can ship thousands of dollars worth of products from several principals to one overseas customer, consolidating the orders at the port and shipping them on one ocean bill of lading.

- *Specialization*: Because the EMC specializes in allied but noncompetitive products, it helps the sales of each individual line. Suppose, for example, that the EMC handles construction equipment. An overseas contractor asks for a price quotation on power shovels but also needs other earth moving equipment. The EMC is in a position to offer trucks, trailers, pneumatic hammers, rotary drills, and related equipment from its various principals, benefiting all concerned, including the overseas customer who deals with a single sources of supply.

- *Overseas travel*: Most EMCs consider overseas travel a normal function of their operations. However, some bill their clients for their routine overseas travel on a cost-share basis, depending on the number of manufacturers represented on the trip.

EMCs are used by both large and small companies, simply because they can undertake exporting more effectively and generally at a lower cost than other channels. Further, it is quite common for exporters to use multiple EMCs. A single EMC may not be able to reach all world markets. In addition, EMCs usually come to specialize by product. Thus, a company that deals in diverse products may use several EMCs.

Interestingly, EMCs usually do not take title, although some EMC do accept title and credit risk and, in some cases even physical possession.

Manufacturer's export agent (MEA): Manufacturer's export agents provide services similar to those provided by the export management company with the exception that they cover limited markets. Further, the contractual relationship is short-term only, from a few months to a year or two. Sometimes the contract applies only to a particular transaction. The MEA acts under his or her own name and receives a commission for services. Thus, while an international marketer might deal with one export management company, he or she would be represented by several MEAs. Because the MEA does not serve the export department of the principal as an EMC does he or she cannot be relied upon to perpetuate business for an export-minded company.

Webb-pomerene association. A webb-pomerene association is formed among competing U.S. manufacturers, especially and exclusively for the purpose of exports according to the Webb-pomerene act of 1918. An agreement in the form of a Webb-pomerene association is exempt from antitrust laws.

The members of a Webb-pomerene association can engage in different international marketing activities to their mutual advantage. For example, they can set prices, combine shipments, jointly undertake marketing research or share information with each other and allocate orders among different members of the association. It is estimated that there are currently over thirty active Webb-Pomerene associations.

Foreign freight forwarders: Foreign freight forwarders specialize in handling overseas shipping arrangements. Their services can be utilized for handling goods from a U.S. port to the foreign port of entry. Occasionally, they may handled inland shipments also. A foreign freight forwarders receivers a discount or fees from the shipping company. For extra services such as a packing, they would be paid by the export manufacturer.

Commission agent: Commission agents represent foreign customers interested in buying U.S. products. They serve as so-called finders for their principals and locate the appropriate goods at the lowest price. The commission agents receive a commission for their services from their foreign clients.

Country-controlled buying agent: This type of agent is an official buyer of a foreign government, seeking to buy designated goods for his or her country. Many developing countries, for example, maintain supply missions in the United States with a number of officers who are entrusted the task of procuring different goods for their countries.

American trading company: The ATC is a new form of indirect channel that can be formed under the Export Trading Company Act of 1982. The goal of this act is to increase U.S. exports by encouraging more efficient provision of export trade services to producers and suppliers alike, by improving the availability of trade finance, and by removing the antitrust disincentive to export activities. Before the Export Trading Company Act. U.S firms were handicapped in forming trading companies because of this legislation, however, there has been an increasing interest among business of all sizes to form trading companies.

Although the act provides a legal basis for the development of ATCs, the shape of their operating characteristics is left in the hands of private business. Because the whole concept of trading companies is new to the United States, it is too early to say what products they normally will handle, how they will be managed, and what services they will concentrate upon. Thus far, agribusiness firms are taking more interest in trading companies than are any other types of business.

Empirical research on the subject indicates that ATCs are likely to be more diversified both in handling products and in geographic coverage. In addition, unlike the EMCs, the ATCs have the potential to be much larger in size and operations. By the same token, decision making in ATCs should be diversified, since the membership would be shared by firms with different backgrounds and cultures.

Indirect through merchant intermediaries

Merchant intermediaries located in the United States serves as middle agents for manufacturers in their export and vendors. Export merchant other manufacturers, export vendors, overseas military market representatives, multinational companies, and the United Nations principally fill this role.

The merchant intermediaries invariably take title to the goods and deal in their own names. They may or may not undertake delivery of the goods, and the services they provide vary.

Likewise, the authority exercised by these intermediaries differs. For example, the export merchant usually has pricing authority but a cooperative exporter does not.

Export merchant: Export merchants buy directly from manufacturers according to their specifications, taking title to the goods. They have overseas contacts through which the goods are sold either to wholesalers or retailers. They assume all the risks and sell in their own names. Their compensation consists of a markup percentage that is based on market conditions. In general, an export merchant resembles a domestic wholesaler.

Cooperative exporter: Cooperative exporter is the name given to any company that has an established system of handling exports for its own goods and distributes products overseas for other manufacturers on a contractual basis. For example, Colgate Palmolive Company has been distributing Wilkinson blades in many international markets. Colgate also acts as a distributor for Pritt Glue Stick and Alpen cereal produced by wheetabix company of England. Lately, colgate and Kao Corporation of Japan had formed a joint venture to manufacture toiletry products in the United States. The products of this venture would be distributed worldwide through the former's distributions network. Similarly, Sony corporation serves as a distributor in Japan for different U.S. and European companies. Through its Sony International Housewares. Sony distributes for such companies as Whirlpool.

Schick Megalware, and Health Company. Kao Corporation of japan, a diversified chemical and detergent company markets Dow Chemical Co.'s corrosion-resistant vinyl ester resin, a type of Fiberglas- reinforced plastic used in industry.

There cooperative arrangements are also called piggybacking. The cooperative exporter may assume the role of an EMC or may just serve as a commission agent for a short period in select markets. The principal asset of cooperative exporters is their experience in dealing overseas as manufacturers themselves. Therefore they are more aware of an sympathetic toward the problems of the manufacturer interested in developing export markets.

Export vendor: Export vendors are companies that specialize in buying poor quality and overproduced goods for distribution overseas. The companies buy goods outright, taking title to them. They ship the goods to one or more countries and sell them through their established contacts. Such intermediaries are useful in times of depressed business conditions in the United States and/or when a company for some reason gets stuck with certain unwanted products. For example, many small U.S. manufacturers used such intermediaries to get rid of goods they produced for the 1980 Olympic Games in Moscow. Since the U.S. did not participated in the games these goods could not be sold in a normal way.

Overseas military market representatives: These are representatives who specialize in selling to U.S.

military post exchanges and commissaries. More than $3 billion annually in consumer goods, not all of them made in the United States, is sold by U.S. military PXs and commissaries overseas. The bulk of this decided what to buy. Commissary managers are restricted by a "brand name contracts" list but still have considerable discretion. All PX and commissary orders are placed through central headquarters in the United States.

The PX and commissary system primarily serves young consumers, among whom ethnic products are popular. Usually, these products are purchased in bulk at top discounts. These representatives generally work for a commission but on occasion will buy on their own for resale. Some representatives handle all types of consumer products; others are specialized.

Multinational companies. Some 5,000 U.S. companies, through overseas subsidiaries, have overseas operations including factories, branch and regional offices, and in some countries elaborate residential compounds for American personnel.

Not all of these companies are committed to buy products from the U.S. Usually they do, however, for three important reasons: (a) their staff is familiar with products from the U.S.; (b) purchasing of major items can be done in the home office; (c) it is cheaper to consolidate purchasing and buy the same brand for all subsidiaries.

The multinational company market generates massive demand for plant machinery, supplies, testing equipment, vehicles, spare parts, process control systems training equipment, computer systems, appliances, office machines, furniture and other goods. Residents of the compounds require all types of household material, entertainment and leisure products.

United nations: The UN's purchasing in spread out among a number of agencies. Some have headquarters in the United states, others in Europe. Any member nation can compete for this business. Each agency is specialized.

The UN agencies themselves do not purchase goods in the same quantities as do projects financed by organizations such as the World Bank. The US agencies often act as advisors rather than actual buyers.

A good example is UNESCO. A $50 million educational development project in Zaire, for instance, may be jointly financed by the government of Zaire, the African Development Bank, and the World Bank, but designed by UNESCO advisors. Purchasing and contracting will be done by the Ministry of Education of Zaire, probably with advice from the same UNESCO team which helped write the specifications.

Other UN agencies operate in much the same manner. A notable exception is UNICEF. UNICEF maintains in Co-penhagen a large warehouse with substantial stocks of basic equipment and teaching aids for primary schools in developing countries.

UNICEF ships from Copenhagen and issues replacement orders as stocks are depleted.

In the United States all UNICEF buying is done through the UN's New York headquarters. To qualify as a vendor one must submit catalogs and specifications, and sometimes samples for evaluation. UNICEF has very strict requirements governing the types of products included on its basic list and carried in its regular inventory.

Direct distribution through agents: A company may deal with different types of agent intermediaries overseas. These agents do not take title to the goods and usually work for a commission. The product involved, and the way it is marketed in the United States, will provide a clue as to who might be employed to undertake overseas distribution- sales representatives, purchasing agents, or export brokers.

Sales representative: These agents resemble a manufacturer's representative in the United States. A manufacturers supplies the sales representatives with literature and samples to conduct sales in a predesignated territory. These representatives usually work on a commission basis, assume no risk or responsibility, and are under contract for a definite period. They may operate on either an exclusive or nonexclusive basis, and they do not handle competing lines. They serve as a good source of market information.

Purchasing agent: These agents are also referred to as buyers for export, export commission house, or export confirming house. They are active in U.S. markets, seeking goods of interest to their foreign principals. Their product quality and price demands stem from the requirements of the principals.

Usually, foreign purchasing agents represent governments or big contractors, either for a specified time or for a particular task. For example, they do not provide continual service and stable volume to vendors. For example, a foreign government might authorize a purchasing agent to buy designated goods in the United State for the completion of a large mill or plant. Once the mill or plant is constructed, the purchasing agent ceases to be active.

Purchasing agents receive commissions from their principals. A transaction with a purchasing agent is completed, as in domestic marketing, with the agent handling all packing and shipping details. A purchasing agent may represent several principals requiring the same goods and may deal with different competing vendors.

Export broker: An export broker brings the foreign buyer and U.S. seller together. Usually, export brokers receive a commission or free from the seller for their services. They take neither title nor possession of goods and assume no financial responsibility relative to the export transaction. Export brokers generally are used in the export of commodities such as grain and cotton. Only rarely is the export broker involved in the export of manufactured goods.

Direct distribution through merchant intermediaries

The foreign merchant intermediaries take title to the goods and sell them under their own names. They may or may not take possession of the goods. They render services similar to a domestic wholesaler. Major types of foreign merchant intermediaries are export distributors, foreign retailers, export, jobbers, and trading companies.

Export distributor: The export distributors purchase goods from a U.S. manufacturer at the greatest possible discount and resell them for a profit. They are especially active in distributing products that require periodic serving. They commit themselves to provide adequate service to the customers through carrying a sufficient quantity of spares and parts, Maintaining facilities, and providing, technicians to perform all normal servicing operations.

Export distributors buy in their own names and usually maintain an ongoing relationship with the exporter. Export distributors have exclusive sales rights in a country or region and receive easy payment terms from exporters.

Foreign retailer: In some cases U.S. manufacturers deal directly with foreign retailers, particularly in the case of consumer goods. For example, Campbell Soup Co. sells its Pepperidge Farm Cookies in japan by directly dealing with a 3,300-store 7-Eleven chain throughout Japan. The contact may be made either through a traveling salesperson or by mail using catalogs or brochures. In many countries, large retailers perform a dual role. While they sell directly to consumers through their own outlets, they also distribute imported goods to smaller retailers. Thus, exports handled by the retailers may receive wide coverage.

Export jobber: Export jobbers determine customer needs overseas and fill them by making purchases in he united States. Some jobbers reverse the process filling needs of U.S. customers by supplying imported products. The jobbers mainly deal in staples, openly traded products for which brand names have little importance.

Trading company: In modern times the so-called trading companies usually are associated with japan. Actually the concept of the trading company is much older. During colonial times many European countries, particularly Britain and France, used trading companies to develop trade with other nations. For example, the East India Company was England's major means to enter India, Similarly, the French trading companies Cle Francaise de I'Afrique Occidentale and Ste Commercials de I'Ouest African were active in Africa.

In Japan, the trading company originated as a commodity dealer that outgrew its wholesale functions. When the country was opened to the West, the trading company primarily served as a buffer between Japanese merchants and foreign business. Then Japan began to industrialize. Having neither raw materials at home nor an empire to exploit, the new industry needed imports. Rather then depend on foreigners, they adapted their trading companies to the task of acquiring the raw materials in addition to moving Japanese goods overseas.

Japanese trading companies have been very successful in promotion Japan's exports. They offer a broad range of services, from marketing research to financing, and present a relatively inexpensive way for the small or medium size firm to do international marketing.

Some major functions of trading companies include trading and distributing, risk-hedging in exchange rates and commodity price fluctuation, domestic and participation in manufacturing, joint venture aboard in resource developments and urban and rural development, and organizing new industries. They only functions that trading companies do not perform are production and retailing, but they may become involved even in these activities through joint ventures.

There are approximately 7,000 trading companies in Japan today, but only about 300 of them are engaged in foreign trade. The six largest trading companies in Japan, referred to as the big Six, are Mitsubishi Corporation. C, Itoh & Company, Nissho—Iwai company, Sumitomo Shoji, Marubeni corporation, a and Mitsui & Company. They had combined sales of over \$375 billion in 1986. They are responsible for bringing in about 68 percent of Japan's imports and shipping out about 44 percent of its exports. These six companies have over 500 offices outside Japan, employing over 15,000 people.

The big trading companies control 56 percent of Japan's foreign trade. Together, they are the main exporters of almost every product that is exported directly by manufacturers. Japanese trading companies have expert knowledge about the lures most attractive to distributors of Japanese exports in all major foreign countries. By contrast, foreign exporters cannot compete so easily in Japan, because they will usually have to sell through a trading company that is part of Japanese group probably making a competing products.

In addition to privately controlled trading companies such as those in Japan many countries have state-controlled trading companies . Such companies are active in counties like those in Eastern Europe where business is conducted by a few government- sanctioned and- controlled trading outfits. In many countries the state-controlled trading companies may be only means of doing business. In many other nations, however, trading companies bridge the gap between Western business style and local cultural practice for conducting business.

Dealing with intermediaries

After exporter successfully locates prospective intermediaries, terms of agreement must be defined between them. A written agreement often avoids later disputes and misunderstanding. However, some companies have a simple agreement, leaving details to be settled when and as questions arise. As long as the intent of both parties is good, it is feasible to work without spelling out every detail in a written document. Yet it is still considered a better alternative to prepare a written contract after the manufacturers has investigated the channel members' overall integrity, financial soundness, community standing, share of the market, and other product lines carried.

In addition to the items shown in the sample agreement, it is desirable to specify that the intermediary will not deal in competing lines, disclose confidential information, or make agreements that bind the exporting firm in any way. Further, the place and time for the title to the merchandise to pass from the seller to the buyer should be clearly stated because of tax implications in the countries of both the exporter and the intermediary,. Finally, the contract should avoid articles that directly or indirectly conflict with U.S. antitrust laws.

Items to include in an agreement with foreign intermediaries

- Name and addresses of both parties
- Date when the agreement goes into effect
- Duration of the agreement
- Provisions for extending or terminating the agreement
- Description of product lines included
- Definition of sales territory
- Establishment of discount and/or commission

schedules and Determination of when and how paid

- Provisions for revising the commission or discount schedules
- Establishment of a policy governing resale prices
- Maintenance of appropriate service facilities
- Restrictions to prohibit the manufacture and sale of similar and competitive products
- Designation of responsibility for patent and trademark negotiations and or pricing
- The assignability or nonassignability of the agreement and any limiting factors
- Designation of the country and state of contract jurisdiction in the case of dispute.

Company owned distribution

An alternative way for a company to arrange for distribution in other countries is to establish its own distribution instead of going through intermediaries. An exporter may choose this alternative for three reasons: to enhance coverage with the objective of increasing sales, to maintain complete control over foreign distribution, and to seek distribution when channels are unavailable.

Foreign company owned channels not only take a long time to establish, but also may not always provide the desired sales results. Difficulties are likely to occur, especially when a change is made in channel arrangements. For example, if an exporter drops existing channels in favor of company- owned distribution, it will face tough competition from them. Further, in many countries it may not be easy to find qualified individuals to serve as salespersons. As a matter of fact in many nations. Japan for example, a company may face insurmountable problems is seeking distribution of its own. Occasionally, a joint venture with a host country business is preferable to a strictly company-owned distribution. The host country business may already have a distribution set-up. The joint venture route provides the exporter an opportunity to enhance control and market coverage without the problems of building channels from scratch.

Channel management

Channel management covers selecting appropriate channels of distribution and making them work. The selection process require decision on distribution structure and choice of specific channel members. Once the selection is made, the goal is to make the channel arrangements work adequately. The requires maintaining cordial relationships and minimizing conflicts.

Channel selection: The channel selection process in international marketing is similar to the one for a domestic situation. Usually, the selection process involves establishing channel objectives and feasible channel alternatives, evaluation of alternatives, and the choice of appropriate channels.

Establishing objectives: The objectives of an international channel of distribution derive from total marketing objectives ion the foreign market. Channel objectives are concerned with a clear-cut definition of the target customers. Implicit in the definition of target customers is the decision about whether the company wants intensive, selective, or exclusive distribution. Intensive distribution is an attempt to reach the mass market, and it requires a broad-based channel structure. Selective distribution is letting a designated channel undertake distribution on a monopoly basis.

Objectives should not only designate the target customers, but also specify the type of service to be rendered to each group of customers. For example, the acceptable time lag between the receipt of an order and deliver of goods should be clearly defined. Similarly, an original equipment manufacturer should state not only the types of services the company intends to make available but also with what frequency.

Establishing feasible channel alternatives: The characteristics of customers, product, intermediaries, competitors, marketing environment, and company's strengths, and weaknesses determine the various possible alternatives for the distribution of a line of products. If the number of customers is large and/ or geographically widespread rather then concentrated, and if they make their purchases in smaller quantities at frequent intervals, the company will have to opt for intensive distribution, that is, a large number of channel outlets. Another factor to be considered here is the desire of the customer to deal with a particular type of channel. For example, the customer in a country may dislike the idea of buying groceries from large supermarkets. In other words, a customer's susceptibility to different selling methods is an important factor to be considered.

A variety of product characteristics have an effect on the selection of channels of distribution. Perishable goods require direct channel. Bulky but inexpensive products can use long channels. Shorter channels are employed when the unit value of a product is high, as in the case of computers, and/or when the product has to be custom-made, like air-conditioning equipment for large building. Proximity to the customer helps in cutting down costs as well as in rendering goods service. Also, products requiring installation and regular maintenance would call for shorter channels of distribution. Most capital equipment talls into this category.

The kinds of channels available constrain channel selection. The company should consider the terms demanded by different channel constituents and evaluate them in comparison with services and benefits provided including factors such as channel location, credit granted, quality of the sales force, warehousing facilities, reputation in the market, outlay on advertising, and overall experience. Consideration must also be given to the demands to the intermediaries from the company. Depending on other factors such as customer and product characteristics, the company will choose those channels that make the maximum impact in the market at minimum cost.

Host country trade practices concerning the distribution of a particular product is another influential variable. It is not necessary to follow competition; however, innovations may not be easily accepted in all countries. Even today many Swiss homemakers prefer buying groceries from mom-and-pop-type outlets.

The environment of the host country constitutes another variable to weight in making a channel selection decision. For example, the economic structure affects the suitability of a particular channels. In free economies, it is common practice to use private agents/distributors who buy and resell at a markup. Most agents/ distributors functions as parts of local companies, which deal in a large number of product lines ranging from candy to sophisticated machine tools. In state-controlled markets, like those of Iraq, Burma, South Yeomen, and Syria, international marketers must do business with state-owned trading companies operating on very low margins that cover physical distribution costs but usually no other necessary marketing activities. In such countries, international marketers often retain the services of private agencies to promote their products to the final consumers. Poor economic conditions may not justify committing the company to excessive fixed costs, and thus distribution through wholesalers may be deemed the best alternative. A depressed economy may also demand cutting down on nonessential services.

Further, cultural conditions might militate against the utilization of a particular type of channel. Consider the factors implicit in the following comment.

Furthermore, the British housewife is not yet freely attuned to the informal aspects of typical supermarket shopping. She likes the modern convenience of the supermarkets but still expects the social relationships, which are traditional among shopkeepers and their customers. As a means to that end, some have scheduled staple buying; fats and oils on Monday; flour and sugar on Tuesday, and so on. That tends to formalize the daily shopping social. Thus, executives of U.S. Food manufacturers doing business in the United Kingdom must realize that British culture assigns a role to the supermarkets that differs from the role in the united States, Successful channel management must take that role into account through the strategies used.

The final factor in evaluating channel alternatives is the company's own strengths and weaknesses in the overseas market. A well-known company of long-standing in the market will tap channels more easily than the new entrant. A financially strong company need not necessarily opt for channels that absorb a part of the distribution costs on inventory, transportation, advertising, and/or training. Similarly a company with a large number of products for the same market could deal directly with the customers.

All these factors serve as a basis for determining the feasible alternative channels of distribution. Generally, the company would have three channel alternatives; selling direct to the customers, selling through intermediaries based in the United States, and selling through foreign distributors. In practice, however, channels in international marketing can be a labyrinth of complicated relationships. For example, the company might sell directly in some countries while employing U.S. based distributors in another country and utilizing overseas distributors in still other cases.

Evaluation of alternative channels: Each channel alternative should be evaluated on the basis of three factors: coverage, control, and cost. Coverage refers to both qualitative and quantitative coverage of customs and is determined by an analysis of customers, including such factors as their geographic locations, sales potential, and service requirements. Usually, customers are grouped into homogeneous categories. Each channel alternative can them be evaluated for different customer segments according to geographic coverage, coverage of big account meeting the needs of different segments, and the like. If deemed necessary, different weights can be assigned to these factors. Often, it will be found that no one channel provides optimum coverage for each segment. Thus, to cater to different segments, the company may be obliged to choose more than one channel.

Control refers to the discretion that the company has, or wants to have, in seeing the goods through to the customers. Dealing with some intermediate agents leaves the company in better control of various activities such as establishing prices, recommending cooperative advertising, and suggesting inventory level. On the other hand, some intermediaries will demand flexibility in pricing, the right to refuse to enter into cooperative advertising freedom in deciding how much inventory they would like to carry, and so forth. I brief, going through the agent/ distributor necessitates sharing control.

If a company wants complete control, it must develop company-owned distribution. Direct distribution, however, requires patience and ingenuity, described in this instance:

Fieldcrest Mill's bed and bath division decided in 1976 export its "boutique" marketing system to western Europe and Japan." It seemed an obvious thing to do" the president explains . "Department stores in those countries were decades behind the United States. They still looked on towels and sheets as mundane products with no fashion pizzazz what ever. And just like a public service to customers."

The firm embarked on a campaign to convince department stores in Europe and japan that they could, like their U.S. counterparts, make money by selling high-fashion towels and sheets. At first there was considerable resistance to Fieldcrest's selling efforts. The owner of a Stuttgart department store flatly rejected the offer of a written guarantee that installation of a Fieldcrest boutique would double the profits generated on that floor space within two years.

But Fieldcrest eventually succeeded in convincing a number of overseas department stores to take fling. Stores in Homburg, Munich, London, and Tokyo agreed to install boutiques in especially favorable locations- usually on the main floor near the cosmetics counters, where customer traffic is heavy. Fieldcrest product the design and even the lighting systems at its own cost. Foreign consumers are now developing a taste for those fashionable U.S. bed and bath products. At London's famed Harrods, the Fieldcrest boutique has become one of the most successful profit centers. As a result of tits boutique concept, Fieldcrest's exports jumped in 1980 by a most respectable 58 percent.

A third factor in evaluating channel alternatives is cost. Direct distribution by the company is usually more costly if the sales base is small. But it gives the company full control over distribution. In the final analysis, a balance has to be struck between cost, coverage, and control. No one factor can be considered in isolation. Probably a composite index should be utilized to measure each channel. The channel with optimum coverage and control at minimum cost would be the obvious choice.

Choosing the channels: After alternative channels have been evaluated, the one most appropriate to the state objective should be chosen. In practice, however, it may be difficult to state the objective in concrete terms for clear matching with each alternative. Thus, subjective judgment becomes important in the final decision. The management should not only consider the implications of the short run, but also allow sufficient flexibility to meet changing requirements. Sometimes a channel is chosen as a stopgap arrangement for a new alternative in the future.

Pros and cons of the use if intermediaries

Independent intermediaries play a significant role in the total global marketing effort of many campaigns. Although even some large companies use intermediaries for seeking distribution in smaller foreign markets or for distribution of certain product lines in larger markets; the distribution through intermediaries is especially important for smaller companies, which generally do not have the scale of operations, financial resources, or experience to operate more directly in foreign markets.

The popularity if this mode of distribution has been attribute to the many advantage that intermediaries provide in foreign markets. A distributor brings immediate new assets to the multinational marketer by providing local market know-how, knowledge, and contacts with little expenditure on the part of the exporter. In the case of selling computers in the Middle East, one writer notes:

Although you know more about the

> product, inevitably the local guy will know more about the market. And make no mistake- market knowledge is more important than product knowledge in getting sales in the Middle East.

Further, the overseas distributor adds to the effective capital available for a company's worldwide marketing efforts., because distributors have funds of their own, as well as local borrowing power that a firm located in another country may not have. The distributor foes these things without a permanent establishment that might lead to unpleasant tax consequences.

Further, intermediaries afford an opportunity for the stocking and sale of a company's product in a new market at negligible cost. The cost of a company owned local operation, involving support staff, office space and equipment, over head, and the like is worthwhile only when a certain volume of business and a certain operating margin are achieved. A distributor may be able to do a good job with a smaller volume by spreading his cost among many lines of products.

The point can be illustrated with this example. A chemical company charges its distributors of textile fibers F.A.S. price less 3 percent. That 3 percent would never cover the costs of maintaining a sales force, local travel expenses, or overhead. But the distributor handles other noncompetitive products-such as textiles machinery- with larger margins. The irregularity of this machinery business is balanced by the steadiness of the fiber sales. Spreading the costs makes it possible for the distributor to carry economically and profitably both lines of goods where neither might be viable separately.

On the other hand, there are some serious disadvantages to using independent distributors. First, the manufacturers has less direct control over an independent distributor than over his or her own employees. Second, there is a risk of violation of U.S. or Common Market antitrust laws when a distributor is being directed, particularly in the area of pricing. Third, the manufacturer may have little contact with, or knowledge of, the retail outlets used by the distributor. Fourth, the manufacturer has little or no control over marketing, sales techniques and credit policies of the distributor. Finally, in some cases, it may be very difficult and costly for the manufacturer to cancel an agreement.

Briefly, then, a company should use distributors in markets where sales volume would not justify its own distribution or when it does not have the staff and know-how to set up its own operations. A firm may or may not change a satisfactory distributor arrangement when local volume could pay the costs of a company's own operation. In some markets, such a volume may never be reached, but in others when it is reached, the distributor relations is retained for any of a host of reasons. Alternatively, the company may acquire or just continue to use the distributor as an adjunct to its own operations in the market.

Selection of intermediaries: Finding reliable distributors is a major challenge for firms entering markets in other countries. There are a number of potential sources of overseas distributors ranging from local trade and banking houses, chambers of commerce, officials of foreign embassies in the United States, and various state and the U.S. departments of commerce. If all of these, the U.S. Department of Commerce provides the most through information. It offers several aids to assist U.S. exporters. There is, however, one important service, titled Agent/Distributor Service. That is designed exclusively to help U.S. firms identify suitable representatives abroad for a fee. The exporters may seek the names of agents and/or distributors abroad who have indicated an interest in handling specific products form the United States.

The following four criteria could be employed to identify suitable intermediaries: financial strength, good connections, the number and kinds of other companies represented, and the quality of local personnel, facilities, and equipment.

Financial strength: Sales in foreign markets take time to mature. Yet the distributors must invest in personnel and equipment ahead of the actual business activity if the organization is to have an effective beginning. Thus, the prospective distributor must be financially sound and should have the strength and will to take the risks involved. Financial strength involves both credit standing and can flow position.

Good connection: In a large number of countries, business is conducted in a personal basis. In many cases, the government is deeply involved in business. Thus, for agent and distributors to be effective, they should be well connected both in private and in government circles. They should be regarded as respectable business persons by all concerned and follow established traditions and practices.

Other business commitments: Information should be gathered on other commitments that the potential intermediary is involved in. For example, someone currently dealing in noncompeting goods and enjoying a good reputation for providing service, handling complaints and problems, and carrying inventory might be a viable candidate. Information on performance can be sought form the companies he or she has been representing. In addition to an encouraging reputation, any experience gained through handling complementary goods would be advantageous in representing the firm's products. However, sound business practice prohibits distributors from handling competing lines.

Personal, facilities, and equipment: The number and quality of the representative's employees, equipment, and facilities should be examined. After all, the reputation of the foreign firm in the host country depends on the activities and behavior of the people representing it. The people should not only be skilled and qualified in their trade but also have good public relations. Further, the distributor's facilities and equipment should be adequate, as well as properly located. If certain equipment is lacking, the distributor should be willing to make additions. Often potential representatives are willing to hire more people and additions. Often potential representatives are willing to hire more people and purchase additional facilities and equipment, if selected. To ensure that the distributor lives to up such promises, these provisions should be specified in the agreement.

The following are additional consideration in the selection of intermediaries:

- Capability to provide adequate sales coverage
- Overall positive reputation and image as a company
- Product compatibility
- Pertinent technical know-how staff level
- Adequate infrastructure in staff and facilities
- Proven performance record with client companies
- Positive attitude toward the company's products
- Mature outlook regarding the company's inevitable progression in market management.

Channel control and performance

Distribution in foreign locales through intermediaries always entails compromise. The compromise involves the loss of control over MNC's foreign marketing operations in exchange for relatively low-cost representation. Although some control must be relinquished to intermediaries even in domestic markets, in foreign markets it is more significant because the firm has no permanent presence abroad. A distributor, the only means of accomplishing all the related tasks-selling , servicing, providing market information-often falls short of the manufacturer's expectations. The independent distributor represents an entiry separate from the exporter, and their goals may not match exactly. Despite the fact that the exporter/ manufacturer lacks full control of foreign distribution, he or she still wants adequate information. This raises the dilemma of how to encourage high performance by channels that are not a part of the firm's own network.

No matter how one looks at it, companies using independent distributors will have great difficulty in controlling them. It is difficult for the exporter to make sales forecasts, set sales targets, and develop customer-contact plans when there is no access to the distributor's book, sales reports, or other records. Thus, the manufacturers should not depend on controls to optimize distributor performance but instead use motivational methods.

A distributor wants to do the best possible job for each of his manufacturers, but he really cannot. So he concentrates (1) where he makes the most money and (2) where he has the least aggravation or the greatest personal pull. The following are some thoughts on how we can build loyalty:

1. Build your distributor with your company: bring him into your picture, discuss future plans as they affect his area with him: seek his advice.
2. Give your distributor an attractive profit margin; try to keep in mind that you want to be in business with him for several years, make him want to continue the relationship.
3. Be sure he has credit terms which make him competitive, or more, so in amount and length of payment.
4. Maintain regular correspondence, and make sure he can clearly understand what you have to say.
5. Make a point of commenting on successful distributors in whatever communication have to say.
6. Keep your obvious control to a minimum as his performance improves, your supervision can be reduced.
7. If financing is needed locally and you have the ability to help, do so if his situation justifies this.
8. Bring the distributor to the United Stated on occasion and let him see what goes on.
9. Offer a scholarship to the children of a successful distributor.

10. Establish a recognition system recognition certificates, cash prize, trips, and so on
11. Make available remembrance items, give away with your name perhaps, if warranted, with his name too.

An empirical study on the subject notes that the performance of an overseas distributor is affected by such relational factors as formalization, standardization, reciprocity, intensity, and conflict. Formalization refers to the extent to which the relationship is agreed upon and made explicit. Standardization indicates the extent to which the established roles and trading routines are followed. Reciprocity means the extent to which the manufacturer and distributor are both involved in decision making, despite the traditional domains of each party. Intensity is the level of contact and resource exchange between the parties. Finally, conflict refers to the level of tension and disagreement between the two parties. The findings of this study strongly recommend that high performance is associated with certain relational characteristics. High performance requires that the two parties:

- Adapt their roles and routines
- Display a commitment to developing business in the market in question
- Exhibit lower levels of intercompany tension and disagreement

In addition, the manufacturer should demonstrate (1) a genuine interest in the foreign market in the overseas distributor, (2) willingness to adapt his or her ways of doing business to be an effective competitor abroad, and (3) an ability to minimize disagreements with the overseas distributor.

Modification of channel

Environmental forces, internal or external, may force a company to modify existing channel agreements. A shift in the trade policy/practice of a country, for instance, may render distribution through a state trading organization obsolete. The experience of companies in the Common Market is relevant here. Multinational companies in EC area have been, in response to the 1992 single internal market program, changing their distribution channels from covering only one national market to covering two or more national markets and serving areas reflection natural rather than national boundaries. Similarly, technological changes in product design may requires service calls to customers more frequently than the current channels can manage, and require the company to opt for direct distribution.

Ordinarily, a company new to the international market starts distribution through intermediaries. The company has little, if any, knowledge of the conditions with the vagaries of the market. For good reasons, therefore, intermediaries are patronized. With their knowledge of the market, they play an important role in establishing demand for a company's products. But once the company attains a foothold in the market, it may discover that it does not have enough control of distribution to make further headway. At this time, modification becomes essential. The perspectives of Japanese companies illustrate the point.

In marketing too, the Japanese have avoided "going global" all at once. When they have an exportable product, they test it out in South East Asia and a few U.S. Cities to learn how to market it abroad. When the situation looks risky, they ask trading companies to do the overseas marketing on their behalf, again so as to prevent their lack of a critical resource- in this case marketing know-how- from becoming a bottleneck to their international growth.

Such caution does not reflect a lack of interest in overseas trade. On the contrary, the company will typically dispatch a high-caliber liaison officer, usually on the CEO's orders, to such places as New York, Chicago and Los Angeles, with a specific mission to develop plans for eventual direct marketing. Many of today's top corporate executives have been on such a mission at some time in their career. The fact that the company may ask trading companies to handle its initial overseas marketing, or may accept OEM deals under well known American or European brands, it likely to reflect a methodical, one-step-at-a-time approach to the long term goal of becoming a global brand.

It is clear in hind sight that such Japanese companies as Canon, Ricoh, Panasonic, and Pentax all had the ambition to become world leaders, but in each cause they started with trading-company, dealer, and/or OEM arrangements. One confident of their product quality and coat competitiveness, they began to address their marketing inefficiencies and gradually to by-pass, first, the trading companies and, eventually, their distributor and OEM partner. Some of them do still accept OEM relationships, but they will soon begin to insist on own -brand marketing also. Dual-brand strategies have in any case been hard to administer in the United States as a result of antitrust legislation, internal administrative complexities, and conflicts over engineering resources allocation. It was because of such difficulties that Pentax left Honeywell and Ricoh left Savin. both aspire eventually to become global marketers in their own right.

Managerial astuteness requires that the company do a through study before deciding to change existing channel arrangements. No matter how long a U.S company has been engaged in business with other countries, there are customs and conditions that may constrain a nonnative firm in establishing its own distribution system. In other words, hurried measures could create insurmountable problems, resulting in loose control and poor communications. Further, the affected intermediary agents should be taken into the company's confidence about future plans and compensated for any breach in terms. Any modification of channels should tally with the total marketing system. This requires consideration of the effect of a modified plan on various ingredients in the marketing mix, such as pricing, promotion, and so on. The managers in different departments should be informed so that the change does not come as a surprise. In other words, care must be taken to ensure that a modification in channel arrangements causes no distortion in the overall distribution system.

Wholesaling in foreign environments

An international marketer interested in overseas distribution must acquire complete knowledge of the existing wholesale and retail patterns of the host country. Such knowledge reveals what sort of distribution is feasible, what economic, social, and cultural factors influence the distribution structure of the country; and what legal and political requirements must be followed. The following two sections examines different aspects of wholesaling and retailing in foreign markets.

Overall wholesalers worldwide perform such functions as purchasing planning transportation storage, financing, information gathering, production planning, risk management, and even management consulting. But in some countries, some of the functions are reserved for manufacturers or retailers or both. Briefly, functions performed by wholesalers vary from country to country. The status and role of wholesalers vary from country to country. In developing countries, they play a crucial role by handling imports as well as products of small, domestic manufacturers and by financing the flow of goods between the producers and retailers. Despite their importance in many developing countries, wholesalers are held in low esteem for two reasons. First, the major economic emphasis in developing countries is on production since goods are scarce in virtually all sectors . Second wholesale trade, like retail, in many countries is dominated by foreigners. The local population, therefore, looks down upon wholesalers as they consider them to be getting rich by exploiting them. For example, in many African counties, like Kenya and Sierra Leone, people of the Indian subcontinent control the trading sector of the economy. About 75 percent of Kenya's retail and wholesale business even today is controlled by Asians . Similarly, the Chinese have been dominant in the Philippines and Indonesia. European companies control a large proportion of Malaysia's and Singapore's trade.

Further, the size of wholesaling operations differs significantly frcm country to country. In Finland, four wholesaling houses handle the major portions of all trade. One of these four houses, Kesko, controls over 20 percent of the market. On the other hand, Japan is known for its myriad wholesalers linked to each other in a multinational arrangement.

Services offered by wholesalers.

Services provided by wholesalers are related to competition. In a country like India, where there are virtually hundreds of wholesalers, the margins are low and the competition is fierce. In such an environment, wholesalers provide a variety of services from financing to inventory maintenance.

On the other hand, the large trading companies usually provide a good service mix, but at a substantial cost to the manufacturer retail. In most industrialized countries, the emerging trend toward vertical integration has squeezed the wholesalers from both sides. The wholesalers, therefore, have tried to streamline by carefully limiting the areas of operation and strictly controlling them. For example, wholesalers continue to be a major factor in Western Europe in food products. Tuus even through Kraft Incorporated distributes in Germany through the company-owned channels, it must provide the wholesalers their commission without receiving any service.

Merchandising policies

Smaller wholesalers usually limit their business to handling a particular family of goods. Whenever they expand, they venture only into related goods. Large wholesaler, however, deal in different products without any underlying relationship among them. For example, Hamashbir Hamerkazi, a large wholesale group in Israel, handles different kinds of products and has interests in twelve large manufacturing firms.

Margins and efficiency

The margin and efficiency of wholesalers depend on the services they provide and the competition they face. Where competition is lacking, wholesalers run an inefficient operation. The wholesaling function simply amounts to an intermediate function for the flow of goods. The inefficiency of operations has no relationship to margins. When the business develops into a monopoly and the goods are in short supply, margins are rather high, despite the low level of services. Keen competition, however, raises the level of services that wholesalers provided without simultaneous improvement in either the margins or efficiency. In brief, wholesaling worldwide is not marked by efficiency, with poor efficiency and ken competition, the margins are meager.

Retailing in overseas markets

Diverse retailing pattern can be observed from country to country, even more than in wholesaling. Retailing in many respects is a localized activity, deeply influenced by prevailing social and cultural norms and government controls. An international marketer should gain as much insight into the retailing practices of the host country as necessary for his or her marketing endeavors.

Worldwide retailing patterns

Retailing operations vary widely in size. Some countries have large stores comparable to those in the United States. In other nations, retailing is a small family business. Harrods of England, Mitsukoshi of Japan and Au Printemps of France are well-known names in retailing, These stores have a large clientele and carry an extensive line of merchandise along the lines of a typical department store in day. Contrast this with retailing in Pakistan and Nigeria, where retailers in a large city number on the thousands and carry one or two lines of goods, serving a very few customers. Relatively speaking, not only is the number of retail stores in the developing countries retailing patter than in the industrialized nations but also by contract the number of customers served is low. As a matter of fact, even among developed countries retailing patterns vary significantly. For example, in 1982 the average sales volume per store was $523,000 in the United States, $40,00 0 in Great Britain, and $182, 500 in Japan.

The level of services that retailers provide to manufacturers varies according to their size. Thus, large retail houses generally carry inventory, render financial help, display and promote merchandise, and furnish market information. On the other hand, smaller retailers would depend entirely on the manufacturers or wholesaler. On their own, they would carry a limited quantity of products and would expect the vendor to provide credit. Promotion and merchandise display material would have to be handled by the manufacturer or the wholesaler.

The smaller retailers carry limited lines of goods in limited variety. Usually, their operations are run inefficiently and their margins are low. On the other hand, large-scale operations are able to achieve economies of scale and infuse professionalism into the operations. Their margins are relatively high, but at the same time so are their services.

An international marketer would have

difficulty dealing directly with smaller retailers. Thus, in nations where retailing is a mom-pop business, the wholesaler becomes important. By the same token, new ideas and innovations overseas at the retail level can be successfully introduced only in countries that have large retail houses.

Theory of international retailing

Any institutional framework in a country is a function of its environment. In the area of international retailing, this thesis is supported by empirical work on he subject. For example, supermarkets were found to be more common and retail outlets much larger in countries with relatively higher GNPs per capita. As a matter of fact, time lags in the development of retailing innovations and improvements appeared similar in length to lags in environmental development. In brief, it can be theorized that the retailing structure emerges from the environmental characteristics of the country. The environmental determinants of retail structure are personal consumption expenditures per capita, passenger car ownership, and geographical concentration of population. The theory of retailing propounded here has a variety of implications for multinational marketers. Arndt says that reported results.

Appear to have important strategic implications for multinational retailers who, more often than not, establish modern retail institutions such as supermarkets and discount stores.....

Conceptual framework may be used by multinational retailers as a base for forecasting the optimal timing to establish retail operations within a new country. The framework may also facilitate decisions regarding the magnitude of investments such as the number of stores to be established in a particular country and their approximate size.

For example, Western capital-intensive mass-market technology clearly is ill-suited to serve low- and middle- income consumers in the Third World. Instead, the traditional labor-intensive food retailer is more suitable for marketing staples to the bulk of the world's population- that is, neither so primitive as to offer no escape from low production and low income, non so highly sophisticated as to be out of the reach of poor people.

Until recently, the transfer of capital-intensive marketing technology was recommended as a solution to Third World problems. The horizontally and vertically integrated systems surrounding institutions known as supermarkets were considered generators of substantial benefits as a result of economies of scale, self service, and a shortened distribution channel. Supermarkets supposedly help to by-pass the public wholesale markets; replace the crowed old-fashioned, noisy, disorderly, dirty but picturesque food stands in municipal retail bazaars and do away with street vendors who cause health and safety hazards in busy downtown areas. In short, the small limited-line retailers of consumer staples- plus the long labor-intensive, and haphazardly coordinated distribution chain- were being arrogantly brushed aside as inadequate, inefficient, and irrelevant.

The experience of the past twenty-five years, however, shows that Western marketing technology is too big and too expensive. It does not create the jobs needed to absorb the rapidly expanding labor force in the Third World, and it is not appropriate for the small firms and business that make up the bulk of the economic activity in developing countries. Further, evidence has been presented that shows competition can emerge when the traditional institutions are well managed.

Global retailing trends

Worldwide, various changes are emerging on the retail scene. Although most changes are limited to advanced nations, different sorts of retailing trends are evident even among developing countries.

Adoption of U.S. Retailing Innovations: Such U.S. retailing innovations as self-service supermarkets. Discount houses, and suburban shopping centers gradually are finding their way into most European countries and Japan. The growth of discounting in West Germany illustrates the points. Stating with the first discount store in 1953, the number of discounters exceeded 1,000 by the 1970s. The new discount house, called *verbraucher market*, are in some cases large than a typical discount store in the United States. Similarly, discounting has taken off in France, where 1960s supermarkets have evolved into hypermarkets, selling not just food but furniture, clothing, and hardware. To illustrate the point, cat food costs 2,80 francs at a hypermarket compared with 5.30 france at a neighborhood shop.

American retailing innovations are also finding their way to developing countries. For example, McDonald's, Kentucky Fried Chicken, Pizza Hut, Burger King, Ponderosa and Wendy's are thriving in many Southeast Asian areas including China.

Even mail order business is catching up. For example, the mail order business traditionally had a shoddy image in Japan. Only such products as contraceptive devices and aphrodisiacs, which reputable stores refused to sell, were convenient to channel through mail. With more Japanese women working and with mail order houses trying hard to improve their image, the mail order business has begun to boom. Well-known companies have began selling jewelry, kitchen utensils, furcoats, baby clothes, and even automobiles by mail. This trend is visible in other countries as well.

Further, the share of business for the large retailers has been increasing as retailing becomes concentrated in few hands. This trend is noticeable throughout Western Europe with the exception of Italy. In Japan, large department stores have captured about 10 percent of domestic retail sales. But their strong market position has been overtaken by so-called supers or general merchandise stores, which handle about 15 percent of retail sales. Self-service and convenience chain stores have also grown rapidly and together hold another 15 percent of the market.

Internationalization of retailing: The growing interest among the large retailers of industrialized countries in expansion overseas is another noticeable change. Sears, Rocbuck & Company has ventured into Mexico, South America, and Spain. J.C. Penney Company moved into Belgium and Italy; Safeway entered Great Britain, Germany, and Australia; Federated Department Stores found its way into Madrid. Likewise, Avon representatives and Tupperware parties have become common in a number of countries. Since 1984, Toys 'R' Us Company has opened megastores in Canda, Britain, Singapore, West Germany, France, Italy and Japan.

The internationalization of retailing, however, is not limited to U.S. business. Harrods, Britain's best -know department store, has branched out into Japan. France's Au Printemps department store opened stores in Japan. Singapore, Saudi Arabia, South Korea, and Turkey. In 1987, it opened its first U.S. store in Denver and plans to open many more in the 1990s. The following is a list of selected European interests in U.S. retailers:

Investor	*Country*	*US Retailer*
Tengelmann	West Germany	A & P
Haniel	West Germany	Scrviner

Rewe-Leibbrand	West Germany	SDC/Furr's
Asko	West Germany	SEC/Furr's
Alberecht	West Germany	Benner-Tea, Albertson
Cavenham	United Kingdom	Grand Union
Promodes	France	Red Food, Houchens
Ahold	Netherlands	First National
Delhaize	Belgium	Food Lion. Food Giant
Otto- Versand	West Germany	Spiegel
Marks and Spencer	United Kingdom	Broods Brothers

Soil marketing: An interesting trend in the developing countries has been the retailers entry into social marketing. For example, retailers in Kenya, Jamaica, and India willingly display and sell contraceptives to support their governments efforts to popularize family planning. This shows the awareness of even small businesses/retailers in developing countries toward the need for social programs and their willingness to participate. It seem that the primitive distribution net-works in developing countries can be counted on for delivery of medically and socially oriented products, ideas, and services. In other worlds, psychologically physically, economically, the retailers are accessible for distribution of such products as health- related foods, over- the-counter medicines, and nutrition and hygiene information, even though each of them may run a small, inefficient operation.

Cooperative retailing: Emergence of consumer retail cooperatives is another trend that deserves mention. Traditionally, consumer cooperatives have been popular in Europe. For example, consumer cooperatives controls almost one- fourth of food sales in Switzerland. Presumably, the tow largest Swiss cooperatives have over one- third of Swiss households as members. In Japan consumers' cooperative union stores, which are nonprofit institutions, are fast emerging as a viable force in food retailing.

The cooperative movement at the retail level, however, is spreading much faster in the developing countries of Asia and Africa. In many countries, government- sponsored cooperative societies have been formed to undertake distribution of essential products. The presence of the cooperatives reduces the volume of trade handled by private retailers and increases the government's control over trade. Interestingly, however, cooperatives do not succeed in many nations because in an economy of scarcity cooperatives are often out of stock of the most needed goods and products. This forces consumers to depend on private sources for their crucial purchases, even though it means paying a higher price.

International franchising

Expansion into international markets represents a major growth opportunity for domestic franchise operations. This section focuses on the entry motivations, ownership practices, marketing strategies, and problems associated with U.S. franchise operations abroad.

The term *franchising* has many connotations ; therefore, its meaning must be delineated in the context of private enterprise where it refers to "a form of marketing or distribution in which a parent company customarily grants in a prescribed manner over a certain period of time in a specified place. An important aspect of a franchise arrangement is the continuing relationship between the parties.

The current growth of the franchise industry is of recent origin and is strictly an American phenomenon. However, franchising as an alternative way of seeking distribution has been known for years. Many years ago, German beer brewers negotiated exclusive arrangements for sale of their brands outside their home market. In the United States, the Singer Sewing Machine Company is credited with the first attempts to establish worldwide franchising operations. Similarly, the Bata Show Company of Czechoslovakia instituted franchising about the same time. Today of course, franchising has expanded to such diverse businesses as fast-food restaurants, business services, construction, hotels and motels, and recreation and entertainment. Overall, franchising accounts for over one-fourth of retail sales in the United States.

Perspectives of international franchising

Companies are primarily motivated by three factors in the expansion of their franchising operations internationally, market-growth opportunities profit potential, and the desire to be known as an international firm. Companies usually initiate franchising in other countries on a limited scale-one or two further expansion. Like the international expansion of U.S business in general, foreign franchising operations usually start with Canada. Western Europe, and Japan. For example, Canada has the largest number of U.S. franchise operations, followed by England and Japan. Fast foods and business services account for over 50 percent of international franchising operations of U.S. firms. In 1987 354 U.S. franchisers operated 32,000 outlets in foreign countries, and their gross sales amounted to almost 86 billion.

Marketing strategy

Firms entering overseas markets by establishing franchising operations must determine if they will follow a standardized or differentiated strategy with reference to product, price, and promotion. Most firms follow a standardized approach, particularly the soft drink and business services organizations. However, same fast food companies have made adaptations in their overseas operations, particularly in the product area, in response to particular cultural habits and customs of different nations.. For example in Japan Denny's serves ginger pork, curried rice, and dishes flavored with soy sauce. McDonald's offers to tomato and beet-root in Austria; in France it serves wine with meals. Diary Queen is attempting to penetrate the Middle East market by adding roti, a type of bread, and a fried vegetable and meat dish to the fare.

Price is duly adjusted to local competition. Promotion also varies, depending on media availability. For example, the use of television in foreign markets is much less popular. The dominant means of promotion are radio and different forms of sales promotions.

Problems with U.S. franchising in other countries

Companies face a variety of problems in their efforts to engage in international franchising. Some are similar to those faced in domestic markets, but differ in intensity and severity.

Other problems may be classified as:

- *Governmental and legal restrictions:* Tax structure, barriers against foreign ownership, and limitation of profit repatriation are some of the problem causing trouble for more than 60 percent of the international franchising firms.
- *Selection of methods of operation*: The method of operation depends largely on the business practice of the host nation, the availability of qualified franchisees, and the availability of capital.
- *Choice of location*: The selection of proper site is a crucial factor in the success of the franchise.
- *Availability of supplies*: Two business inputs- qualified personnel and food materials- face scarcity problems in Japan and Europe.
- *Adjustment to local tastes and customs*: Recognizing local traditions and tastes is of

utmost importance. Culture, habits, consumer behavior, and desires vary widely from nation to nation.

- *Operational problems*: Once opened the outlet faces problems that threaten its continued existence. The two prevalent challenges facing international franchising have been competition and the ability to adapt to local conditions while maintaining one's uniqueness. Monitoring the customs and habits of the host country is always necessary in order to discover or anticipate changing trends.
- *Limited expansion opportunities:* The international franchising industry has been a relatively recent development. Progress has been rapid, however, and the large U.S. franchisers all have outlets in foreign nations, with plans for further expansion. Analysis indicate that although there are difficulties that must be overcome, expansion opportunities do exist and the future of international franchising appears optimistic.

International franchisers must ascertain the basic practicability of transporting their business system to a foreign country and engage in a through market research study before attempting to expand internationally. Many American firms stumble because of their mistaken assumption that what works at home will work overseas as well. The success of international franchising will probably depend upon the ability to adjust to a culture with different attitudes, values and beliefs.

Future trends

For numerous reasons, the international franchising operations of U.S. corporations should grow at a fast pace in the 1990s. First, as the people in Western Europe and Japan move away from downtown areas into suburbs and as more and ore women start working, the fast-food industry should prosper. Second, there has been a gradual break in the tradition of going home for lunch, particularly in France, Germany, England, and Scandinavian countries. his is attributed to tightening of working hours, forces by the need to increase productivity, Third the rise in discretionary income in Europe and Japan has enhanced the need for convenience foods. For example, companies like McDonald's and Kentucky Fried Chicken are showing annual sales increases of 50 percent a year. Fourth, franchising permits a substantial involvement of the local entrepreneur right from the emerging developing tential because it permits mass distribution, involves native businesspersons, and offers a standard product/service at a price trimmed by economies of scale. In conclusion, the future of franchising operations in the international markets appears promising, and more and more companies may seek new foreign market entry franchising.

International physical distribution

International physical distribution encompasses the logistics or movements of goods across countries from the sources of supply to the centers of demand. In other worlds, it is concerned with getting the right product to the right place at the right time, in good condition and at reasonable cost. Warehousing, transportation, and inventory are the major components of physical distribution. The final purpose of physical distribution activity is to provide adequate service to the customer. For satisfactory performance of this function, the various components of PD should be properly integrated for worldwide distribution.

Importance of international physical distribution

The importance of international physical distribution is illustrated by Japan. Two large metropolitation areas in Japan-Tokyo and Oska-consume approximately 85 percent of all gaslone sold in Japan. The physical distribution system for a particular oil company serving Japan is made up of four different levels of intermediary agents, a nation wholesaler, at regional wholesaler, a local wholesaler, and a retailer. The gasoline is physically delivered to the national wholesaler, who then has it delivered to the regional one, them on to the local one, and finally the retailer. There is nothing odd about this distribution system until one stops to consider that all channel members are located within the same metropolitan area. It would be considerably more convenient and far cheaper to ship the gasoline directly from the oil company's tanks to the retailer. Because of the cultural environment in Japan, it may not be entirely feasible to streamline this distribution system, Nevertheless, the example services to indicate that, evaluating and implementing an alternative system, the delivery cost of the gasoline could be lowered. For example, an American manufacturer trying to penetrate the Japanese consumer goods market satisfied the cultural requirements by routing the paperwork through various levels of appropriately compensated intermediaries while distributing the product itself directly. Distribution is a marketing area that management might have a tendency to view as a so-called cost sink without realizing that considerable savings can be achieved by proper analysis and revision of distribution systems.

The physical distribution of goods is usually accepted as it is. It is rarely realized that this is one area that offers a great potential for increasing efficiency. In no other function is there as much waste duplication, and indifference as there is in the moving of goods from one country to another.

Even in a strictly domestic business with many plants, warehouses, and markets, physical distribution is considered to be a difficult function. Added to this in the international context are the complexities of national borders, customs of trade, tariffs and duties, carrier performance, nationalism, monetary exchange, and the necessity of filing numerous documents.

Management of international physical distribution

The three important aspects of physical distribution are warehousing, transportation, and inventory management. The basic decision to be made concerning warehousing are how many warehouses of what size a company needs and in which country they should be located. The decision on warehousing requires information such as where the firm's customers, both current and potential, are geographically located around the worlds; what is the pattern of their current demand, and what demand pattern is likely to emerge in the future; and what level of customer service should be followed. The last item refers to the number of days within which the customer order would be filed. Often customers are categorized based on their importance for the company. The service level is varied in different based on their importance for the company. The service level is varied in different categories. All this information is analyzed before making the warehousing decision.

The transportation decision mainly involves choice of a model of transportation for shipping the goods both internationally and locally within a foreign nation. This decision is affected by such factors as the availability of transportation, nature of product, size of shipment, distance to be traveled, type of demand and cost of different shipping alternatives.

Inventory management deals with stocking inventory to fill customer orders. It involves two decisions- how often to order in a given period and how much to order. The costs involved with these decisions are inversely related. For example, if too may orders are placed in a year, the ordering costs go up. On the other hand, if large quantities are bought at a time, the total number of orders is reduced and hence the total ordering cost, but the costs of carrying large purchases go up. Thus, an optimum point must be found for the number of orders and the size of each order. This can be figured by using different forms of informational inputs and an appropriate mathematical formula.

So far the three aspects of physical distribution have been discussed separately . For an integrated decision on international physical distribution, however, these three aspects should be considered simultaneously. This amounts to considering physical distribution as a system with thee components- warehousing transportation, and inventory management.

The logic of applying a systems approach to physical distribution is simply. Because the costs involved in administering warehousing, transportation, and inventory functions are interrelated, that they must be considered simulatenously for effective decision making. For example, if the number of warehouses is increased, transportation costs will decrease but inventory costs will increase- inventory will have to be duplicated at more places. Similarly, if an attempt is made to decrease inventory costs by cutting soen inventory levels, transportation costs will go up. Obviously, an optimum decision mandates that all relevant costs be considered in an integrated fashion and in relation to the desired service level.

International physical distribution: An example

Illustrated here are the highlights of Eastman Kodak Company's international physical distribution arrangements as an example of how a large MNC moves goods internationally. For Kodak, proper distribution means getting the right product to the right place at the right time, in good condition, and at a reasonable cost. To achieve this, Kodak has developed a highly integrated worldwide distribution system.

International organization: Sophistication, coordination, and cooperation are required in order for Kodak to provide a wide range of products manufactured in both the United States and foreign factories to all of its corporate installations around the world. The center of Kodak's organization in this important area is the International Distribution Operations Committee. The committee pervade a focal point for the distribution Division interface with the International Photographic Division and also develops and evaluates new ideas in the export area.

Inventory management: Kodak's inventory management system consists of two subsystems. The automatic replenishment subsystem determines the timing and amount of an order to be placed with one of the manufacturing companies. If stock is below a predetermined reorder point, the system prepares a replenishment order that is reviewed by the local planning department, thereby eliminating the time the stock planner usually spends in clerical review of the product line and leaving more time for true planning. In addition the system automatically establishes control points used in the reorder cycle, which is the second part of the inventory management process. This system provides each of Kodak's computerized foreign facilities with an effective and efficient means of maintaining properly balanced inventories.

The results of the dual process are replenishment orders sent to Kodak manufacturing plants from one location to another. For the last five years, transmission of computerized information has been relayed over telephone lines in Northern Europe among six nonmanufacturing companies. One large computer in Sewden have serviced smaller computer system in Denmark, Norway, Finland, Belgium, has Holland. Each might, replenishment orders from these six Kodak companies are transmitted from Sweden to New York and then to Rochester. By reducing lead time, inventories at the ordering locations can also be reduced. In attempting to maintain a proper worldwide balance of inventories, the main considerations are efficiency, accuracy, and timing.

Shipping: Kodak's General Transportation group coordinates product movement from Rochester to foreign markets. Kodak's goods are shipped to New York City by truck and then by either ocean or air freight. In-transit time accounts for the majority. Therefore, general transportation must try to make this time as short as practical, and the product as safe as possible, during the in-transit time interval. Also, they must schedule the timing and method of shipment so that Kodak gets the best possible rates for the service it uses.

Warehousing: Kodak's international distribution system is based on the assumption that the supplying factory has sufficient inventory in its distribution center to fill the order. This is the most important link in the entire chain of events. Along with its marketing and manufacturing divisions, Kodak's distribution division is responsible for ensuring that the factory distribution centers will have the product when it is needed. This means that Rochester must maintain close contact with the international marketplace to see that sales requirements for the foreign market are properly incorporated into the marketing, distributing, and manufacturing chain of events.

This function is performed by international Estimating, and an international information system has been developed to aide them in the task. This information system consists of three parts. Weekly information is provided to international Estimating for a select number of key items. The second part generates monthly stock and product sales data in card format from each of the international companies to the supplying factory. The final portion of the system operates on a quarterly basis and is involved with medium- term forecasting. The last step help International Estimating in establishing sales estimates to present to marketing as the first step in the production scheduling process.

10 The Role of Promotion in the Future

This chapter deals with the future of promotion. It is particularly important that we understand the directions promotion will take, given the tremendous susceptibility of the field to change. In fact, promotional decision making has always involved being cognizant of both the present and the future in order to be effective. Promotion in the 1990s will emerge out of the environmental conditions and decisions of he 1980s. The following scenario was posited by Edward Cornish, president of the World Future Society.

Imagine a man coming home from a hard day at work, plopping down in front of the TV screen, pushing buttons, and going on a wild buying spree, Bedazzled by all the goodies, he spends every nicked in his bank account and borrow up to his credit limit. He goes broke just sitting in front of his TV set. But before he declares bankruptcy-in consultation with an electrönic attorney-help suddenly appears. Marketing researchers have sponsored a video contest in which people qualify for the prize by evaluating various products shown on TV. Our friend is declared the winner and his bank account is instantly replenished. Over-joyed, he signals his lawyers to call off the bankruptcy proceeding, and he pays off all his bills. From the depths of despair, he is lifted to ecstasy, and all this has happened in the two hours since he got home from work.

Clearly, the technology exists today that would make this scenario possible. What remains unanswered is, first, how this technology will satisfy the needs and wants of the consumer, second, what environmental factors will influence the consumer, and how; and, finally, how can and will marketing respond to these factors in order to make the company more successful? These are real issues that any thinking brand, product, or promotion manager must confront every day and must project into the future. This final chapter provides some initial insights into the major factors that may influence the role promotion will take in the decades ahead.

We will first look at the environmental factors and how they might change in the future, then we will look at the changes that will take place with the consumer, and finally, we will examine the changes that will occur in the nonpromotional elements of the marketing mix. The chapter will conclude with a discussion of how these factors will influence the promotional mix of the future.

Future environmental factors

There are literally thousands of environmental

factors that have had an impact on promotion, are currently influencing promotion, and will influence promotion in the future. Some of these factors will he constant influence while others will vary in their impact. For instance, the influence of moral values on promotion appears to be diminishing. Conversely, the influence of technology is growing dramatically. The discussion that follows delineates environmental factors that appear to be salient in the future. The list is neither comprehensive nor is there any claim of total accuracy.

Technological advancements

Few would disagree that the most dramatic advances in our society during the next two decades will be in the area of technology-particularly, communications technology. Advances such as interactive cable, fiber optics, talking computers, satellite transmissions, videotex, and other technologies will radically change the ways in which products, services, and ideas are marketed in the next twenty years. As a result, electronic communications will make marketing global, instantaneous, and highly individualized by the year 2000. This will mean, for example, that the time between the first identification of a need and the actual sale and consumption of the good will be compressed to the point where it will seem to have disappeared.

New communication services could lead the way to a variety of technological systems that solve many of the world's most pressing problems.

For example, microprocessors could increase the efficiency with which energy is used, enabling people to keep their homes warn and drive their automobiles with far less expenditure of fuel than is now required. Or, better communication techniques may enable the world to curb its population growth, thereby averting starvation in third world nations.

Computer acceptance will also advance tremendously during the 1980s. By 1990, more than half of American homes will have personal computers that will be used for family record-keeping, computer mail, and access to commercial data banks. More people will be able to work at home and communicate rather than commute to their jobs. Many people will correspond by computer message systems, and use the computers to advertise their homes for sale, locate jobs, shop, and bank. With the computer system, it should be possible to offer something for sale, conclude the sale, and transfer the money to a bank account within five minutes of your decision to sell it.

Although there are a great many communication and computer technologies that will affect promotion in the next twenty years, Edward Cornish mentions live that be considers particularly important.

1. *Cable TV*—Of particular interest are the parabolic microwave antennae which follow consumers to receive virtually every satellite signal in the world, representing the ultimate in fragmented media.

2. *Telephone*—The declining cost of long-distance calls combined with new service will mean that telephone marketing will become more selective, less costly, and less offensive to the consumer.
3. *Talking chips*—Computers will be talking to a lot of people in the 1980s, and many of these computer messages should be of great interest to the market.
4. *Electronic information systems*—These systems will provide information on restaurants, departments stores, and all kinds of other services, and allow consumers to identify more accurately the products best suited to their needs.
5. *Home of the future*—One development already occurring is the media room, in which a person can pass countless hours drenched in visual and auditory sensations.

Economic factors

In retrospect, this county's incredible economic boom, stretching for almost thirty years from the late 1940s to the mid-1970s, was a unique period in world history. It was the greatest economic boom the world has ever known, and the United States was the pacesetter. It is astonishing to think that in the 1950s one American worker's productivity was equivalent to that of four Japanese workers or two German workers. When we think about this in comparison to the present and what the Japanese are doing to us in cars, TV sets, videotape, steel, and computer memory chips, it is sobering. It may be the result of two forces moving in opposite directions.

The first forces is the fact that our rate of increased productivity has been going down. For example, from 1948 to 1965 it was increasing at a rate of about 3.3 percent a year. Then, for the next twelve years, from 1965 to 1977, the rate of increase was cut in half. Up to the present moment, the rate of increase has disappeared and there has been some actual slippage. The second force is that while our productivity has deteriorated, the challenge from abroad has moved in the opposite direction. They are getting better all the time.

These factors have produced an era of economic instability. Esteemed economist Paul McCracken did an analysis of economic stability for the whole century, excluding the way years and the years of the Depression. he came up with the calculation that the average increase in standard of living costs over the full scope of the century, up to the late 1970s, had been 2 percent, that is a 2 percent increase in the cost of living per year. The average century-long rate of unemployment had been 4.7 percent. So clearly, the stability we enjoyed after the war was not unusual. What is unusual is the instability that we are going through now, and various calculations show the extent to which we are now borrowing from the future. Although we now have some abatement of our inflation because of the recession, the extent to which we are living off our savings and other accumulated resources makes it almost inevitable that inflation will reoccur.

Today's economic instability is not the ordinary boom/bust cycle, but a symptom of an apparent underlying weakness. It is clearly the kind of economy that none of us can fully understand but that is impinging on our lives in a disturbing way, resulting in the fact that by the beginning of this decade. Americans began to experience an actual decline in their standard of living. This, quite naturally, affects our outlook toward the future. It means that many Americans feel that being able to attain the American dream-a new home and automobile-is well beyond their reach.

Legal and ethical factors

perhaps the only things that can be said for sure about the legal and ethical elements impinging upon marketing is that there will be more of them and they will be even more difficult to understand. Although there has been some talk recently about the need to deregulate business, this is not likely to occur. The primary reason for increasing government intervention in the marketplace is simply that more and more of the nation's citizens want protection from industry abuses. They want manufacturers to provide safe, study, and well-designed products that are fairly prices. They also want the negation process, which includes the finance charge, the warranty, and other supporting services to be provided adequately and efficiency. Furthermore, in the production of this product, they would like our environment kept unpolluted. Finally, people also want to be guaranteed that the business is conducting itself in an honest and ethical manner.

Another force behind increased government regulations is the growing sophistication of the natural and social science. Today there are forecasting techniques that can tell the public more about the long-run implications of what the firm does. Thus, we know that the preservatives used in a large variety of foods have been found to be associated with several types of illnesses. As a result, manufacturers of processed meats have dramatically changed their manufacturing procedures.

The final reason for more regulation in the 1980s is that many laws and regulatory agencies have stimulated teal growth in the affected industries. Perhaps the best examples is the banking industry in this country. As a result of the economic collapse in 1929, a whole set of banking legislation was passed that protected the interest of the customer and made banking much more profitable. Since that time, and most recently in 1981 and 1982, major legislation was passed that gave the banking industry a whole new set of products and marketing opportunities. The success produced in banking has made the attitude of other industries far more positive toward government intervention. Consequently, marketing firms have developed technical staffs that are intimately familiar with all the aspects of existing and future regulations. These firms are not only keeping up with legislation, but they are also attempting to influence it through lobbying efforts as well as by incorporating it into their long-range strategy. All these trends will continue.

The consumer of the future

The consumer of the future will likely be tougher, more volatile and more affluent; have a wider range of individual tastes and preferences; and will probably be more unpredictable. Family spending will probably follow a pattern of conspicuous conservation dictated by economic necessity while changing American life-styles. Four basic factors will determine spending in the future; energy conservation, alternations in economic and demographic patterns, new technologies, and shifting values. We will discuss two of these factors-demographic patterns and shifting values.

Demographic patterns: There will be several demographic shifts during the next decade. According to the new projections from the Census Bureau, America's population will grow to 250 million in 1990 and 268 million by 2000. However, according to the Bureau's middle projection series, based upon realistic assumptions about fertility, life expectancy, and immigration; the United States population will peak at 309 million in 2050 and then begin to decline. According to the middle series projections the total number of annual births will climb from 3.6 million in 1981 to 3.9 million in 1988 and then decline. Never again will this country reach the 4 million annual births of the baby-boom years. In conjunction with this trend, the median age of the population will rise from thirty years in 1980 to thirty-six years in 2000 as the baby-boom generation ages and fewer children are born.

There are a number of important implications associated with the aging of America. For example, in the 1930s the dependency ratio was 9 to 1. Nine people in the work force were supporting every one who had retired. Now it's three to one. By 1990 it will be two to one. This fact sill put a tremendous burden on our society and on the relations between the generations. In addition, people will be retiring at an earlier age and living longer. It is conceivable, that for a large percentage of the population, that some people will be retired a greater number of years than they work. Opportunities for second careers will be likely.

Another implication is that the older population will also dictate the social priorities in the United States. In the 1950s, three out of every four voters had children in school. That fact set the domestic agenda in a striking way; building schools, shopping centers, sub-urban homes. Now, only one out of five voters have children in school. What programs will the government support in the years ahead?

Shifting values: For the past twenty-five years, a new type of social morality has been evolving in this country. An illustration of this new morality is the increasing number of people filing for personal bankruptcy even though they have assets. The stigma attached to this symbol of personal failure appears to be diminishing. We also see this new morality as it relates to sex and marriage, to life-styles, to personal behavior in the work place, and to the pluralism of values. But it is a phenomenon that, particularly in the new economic climate, is changing its shape and will have a different meaning in the 1980s than in the past.

The traditional moralists say, "sacrifice for others". The new morality stresses concern with self. Tradition says, "save for a rainy day." The new morality says, "live in the present." In traditional morality, success was measured by external cues; owning a home, going to a good school, moving up to an even bigger car, and other status symbols. Under the new values, success is measured by inner intangibles, living the full, rich life, seeking opportunities for inner growth, fulfilling one's potential. The old morality stressed the one right way-man as provider, woman as supermom and superwife, marriage, family, and respectability. The new morality stresses choice and pluralism.

There are some statistics that clearly reflect some of these changes. The University of Michigan, for example, did a study over twenty years ago that showed that 80 percent of the public felt that anyone who wasn't married was either sick or a deviate-something was wrong with them. This study was repeated eighteen years later, and the rate had gone from 80 to 26 percent. Similar evidence is found with other issues.

Gallup showed that disapproval of a wife working if her husband could afford to support her was at the 78 percent level. Now it is 25 percent. It is okay to be a working wife. It is also okay to live together without marriage. In 1960, 400,000 couples were in that blissful state. Now the number exceeds 1,000,000. The divorce rate among couples that have been married more than twenty years has quadrupled since 1965. It was become morally acceptable to be single and have children according to 75 percent of the public. Today, one out of six births are out of wedlock, a 50 percent increase in a decade.

Daniel Vankelovich, has carefully monitored our societal changes for several years, and concludes that the American public has decided that;

> genuine self fulfillment requires commitments that endure over long periods of time, and that the expressive and sacred domains can be attained only through a web of shared meanings that transcend the self conceived as an isolated physical object.

This new type of personal commitment embraces greater autonomy for both men and women; more freedom to choose one's own life-style; life weaved as an adventures as well as an economic chore; leisure; self-expression and creativity; a greater concern for both heritage and the future; a more caring attitude; and a larger place for the awe, mystery, and sacredness of life.

Professor William Lazer, a noted futurist, cites thirteen life-style changes that will occur in the 1980s and 1990s;

1. Living my own life,
2. Enhancement of psychological self,
3. Enhancement of physical self,
4. Cosmopolitanism,
5. Security and risk avoidance,
6. Restlessness and impermanence,
7. More leisure and discretionary time,
8. Changing perspectives of work,
9. Escaping from it all,
10. Convenience and immediate gratification,
11. Product dominance,
12. Secure and comfortable living spaces, and
13. Different forms of home ownership.

Whether all these changes will occur and to what extent they will occur is yet to be seen. However, it is clear that the consumer of the future will be different.

Trends in nonpromotional marketing factors

The interaction between promotion and other marketing factors is both real and dynamic. Two types of marketing factors are particularly importance to promotion. The first incorporates the three other marketing mix functions, that is, product, price, and channels of distribution. The second includes the major change that is taking place in respect to the philosophy of marketing-societal marketing.

Product: Product will remain the primary interest of marketing in the decade ahead. As the consumer becomes more discriminating and intelligent about product choices, marketers will become more pragmatic in respect to product design and aesthetics. More emphasis will be placed upon the utilitarian aspects of the product. This consumer orientation will put more pressure on technical research, product testing, and quality. Finally, the product will reflect a societal responsibility for resources conservation and product durability.

Pricing: With the increased cost of borrowed money, pricing will be looked at as the major sources of return on investment. This will be particularly difficult given the consumer's increased sensitivity toward high prices and the government's increased desire to set more pricing and prcfit guidelines. Consequently, firms will have to employ unique pricing techniques to generate higher product turnover and a competitive advantage. Special pricing techniques such as multiple unit pricing, couponing, and rebates will grow in popularity.

Channels of distribution: Increased fuel and energy costs will justify a great deal of innovation in distribution and will force more attention on getting the product to customers with the best possible services and the least amount of transportation costs. Warehousing and inventory control will be heavily emphasized. Furthermore, mangers will be much more careful in determining basic channels of distribution to be used in marketing products and services and more critical in selecting individual establishments for distributing goods. For many products in high demand and short supply, selective distribution will be much more widely utilized. With the further development of computer technology, shopping through at-home systems may mean that fewer stores will be required and that the variety of products will be quite limited.

Societal marketing: Today's and increasingly tomorrow's, socially responsible business firm will recognize its duty to respond to the needs and desires of stockholders, employees, suppliers, consumers, and the general public and not just to one or two of these groups at the expense of the others. Marketing, too, must be expanded to included a number of societal elements. Marketing will be more concerned with human needs, not those met solely by products and services but those of humans living in a delicate societal and ecological setting. Marketing will more and more accept the obligation to advocate clean air, pure water, and adequate housing and to promote conservation and meaningful life-styles. Also, through the continued implementation of marketing techniques, socially desirable goals such as population control, improved racial tolerance, and increased support of education may be more readily attained. Finally, societal marketing will mean that a business must assess not only the profitability of its actions, but also the overall effect that those actions have on society.

Promotion in the future

Now that we have discussed the major factors which will influence promotion in the decades ahead, it is appropriate to examine what those changes may turn out to be. There appears to be some general changes that will occur within all phases of promotion. For instance, it is likely that the emphasis in promotion will shift from stimulating demand to getting the greatest possible benefits from the product, making it last, and curbing the consumer's demand for more and more. Supportive services such as warranties, guarantees, and repair will be re-evaluated both in form and content, and certainly will be a more integral part of every promotional effort.

The shortage economy of the 1980s and 1990s may witness a decline per dollar of sales in the actual outlays for all promotional efforts. Yet, product branding and promotional expenditures for market penetration and product positioning will continue to be the focus of many marketing firms' promotional efforts. In addition, marketers are likely to be more specialized and segmented in the future, requiring specialized forms of promotion.

Advertising

If advertising is to maintain effectiveness, several adjustments will need to be made. Advertising will have to become more rigorous in its attempts at self-regulation. Unless the advertising industry can gain the trust of the government and the consumer, the cost of developing acceptable advertisements will become unbearable. Many advertisers will take their case directly to the consumer; telling the consumer what the corporation does; telling them why it does it, and so on. This dialogue between the advertising industry and the many governing agencies must take place if advertising will survive.

As the consumer is bombarded by more and more messages through more diverse media, developing fresh, creative advertisements will become difficult. Advertisements to continuously refresh themselves. In order to do this, advertising will have to monitor the interaction between itself and its various publics. We must know how ads affect individuals-how they react-and what changes work best.

Media planners in the 1980s will have their hands full trying to come to grips with the total audience that will become more and more splintered. Consequently, media planning will become a more complex task. Media goals will become more precise-more one-on-one-with the target consumer defined in much greater detail than today. Media will respond to fundamental demographic changes in society such as working women, singles, the elderly, and special hobbies. Geographic targeting of commercials is also a possibility.

The cost of media will be unrealistic by todays standards. A thirty-second announcement in a successful prime-time television program costs about $120,000 today. By 1990, a comparable spot will cost $342,000, with a smaller audience. These apparently outrageous rates will not be confined to television. A four-color full page in Time Magazine will probably be pushing $200,000, while playboy will be asking nearly $120,000. It will become more important than ever to get every ounce of effectiveness out of each dollar. A vast amount of testing and trial of new media will occur in the 1980s. We will learn more about how frequency works, the effects of flighting, and media effectiveness in general. All media personnel will require a greater understanding of computer technology.

Creative approaches currently used in advertising will also be reappraised. For example, commercials using a slice of life of humorous vignettes will appeal to all age groups and all kinds of people. However, as the medium become specialized, perhaps emotional advertising that reaches out and touches various audience segments will become more popular and a more appropriate form of carrying the selling message. If global satellite transmission becomes a reality, the same commercial may become more graphic to overcome the language problems. Also, videotaping of programs in the home means that the commercial included in the program will be seen more often, perhaps suggesting changes to reduce the irritating effect of some commercial approaches. Another new vista for creative people will open when syndicated advertisers put syndicated programs on the air on such topics as pet care, car care, and so on.

Promotional strategies will continue to view sales promotion with increasing importance during the 1980s and 1990s. As both direct and indirect competition grows, the battle for shelf space, position, and the consumer's attention at the point of purchase will grow proportionately. This is the domain of sales promotion. Increased monies allocated to sales promotion will require these departments to be better managed. New demands will include more basic research, more short-and long-range planning, and better measures of effectiveness.

This new emphasis on sales promotion will produce new promotional innovations. Some of these will come directly from the manufacturer to meet specific needs or events. Others may be produced by the sales promotion managers themselves. Technology available soon includes the electronic delivery of coupons through a device attached to a television set, and talking check-out registers and vending machines. Sales promotion innovations are only as limited as technology itself.

An area of sales promotion that will experiences tremendous growth and change will be direct marketing. This area includes those techniques which direct the customer or prospect to produce some type of immediate action. Factors that will increase the popularity of direct marketing are;

1. Electronic mail transmission,
2. Two-way TV communication,
3. Customized catalogues, and
4. National and international retailers.

Public relations

maintaining the goodwill of the various publics will continue to grow in importance, and public relations will remain the major means for reaching this goal. As the size of the units of human organization continues to expand, as the interactions between groups of people become more important to all, and as the communications media multiply, a need is created for the services of interpreters and advocates of new viewpoints.

Two general trends are projected for the field. First public relations will become more specialized in its application. Public relations specialists will exist for financial institutions political candidates, environmental groups, colleges and universities, and so forth. Second, public relations people will adopt a more scientific approach to their profession. This will include many of the research tools employed by advertisers.

Personal selling

In the years ahead, as management focuses increasingly on profits rather than sales, salespeople will be under intense pressure to be productive. With todays accounting systems, a salesperson can be readily analyzed as an independent profit-and-loss center. Also, rising costs will dictate new trends in sales meetings, shows, and conventions. Time and territory practices will be revamped, sometimes completely, as companies try to cope with costs and energy constraints. Population changes will also affect the availability of sales personnel and the career paths of mangers themselves.

Index